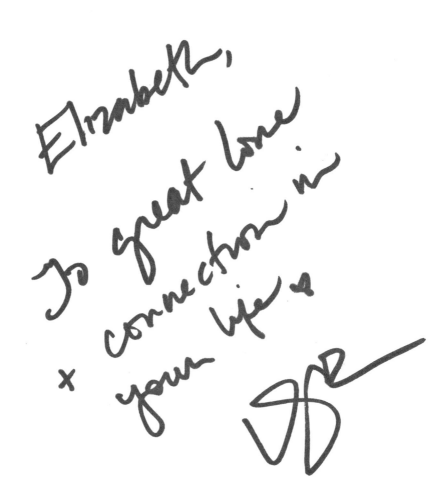

Elizabeth,

To great love
& connection in
your life ♥

x

D1601561

The Cosmology of Love

70+ Ways to Experience Greater Love

By Laura Smith Biswas

What is a Cosmology?
A theory about the origin and nature of the universe.
Oxford Dictionary

The Love Mandala Publications
1146 N. Central Avenue 312
Glendale, CA 91202

Copyright © 2018 Laura Smith Biswas.
www.TheLoveMandala.com

Cover Design by Stephanie Miller
Illustrations by Tamara Brown

Library of Congress Cataloging-in-Publication Data

Biswas, Laura Smith

The Cosmology of Love: 70+ Ways to Experience Greater Love / Laura Smith Biswas

ISBN-13: 978-0692886007

ISBN-10: 0692886001

I. Love 2. Relationships

Dedication

I dedicate this book to my family - Sugata, Anjali, Alia and Kalika who taught me so much about what it means to love, where I need to grow to experience more love and the variety of ways of loving that are possible. If not for them, I would not have asked the question that led to the writing of this book. In addition, I would be remiss if I did not acknowledge how much I learned from Timothy Aguilar who started me on my own journey to self-love.

Contents

Acknowledgements

A special thank you goes to Tamara Brown of Opal Moon Henna for creating all the wonderful symbols used in this book. I'm very grateful to Sabu Quinn for editing the book and providing valuable feedback throughout. In addition, much appreciation is due to Stephanie Miller for guiding the publishing process and Kellee Rutley for encouraging the creation of The Love Mandala revolution that inspired this book.

Foreword

Love is in the details. I first met Laura Smith Biswas in a yoga studio aglow with candlelight. Laura approached me at the end of a seminar I was leading on the hidden power of intimacy and transported me, in mere seconds, to an intimate, loving space – in the middle of a crowded room. The kind of warmth and focus Laura exudes can be found only among the very few who have traveled long and hard within themselves to discover the source and meaning of love. Love that seeks to understand. Love that is boundless.

Most see love as a static thing. You either feel it or you don't. For those, love remains inert or, eventually, dies away. There are others, who see love as a living thing. Something that thrives under the right conditions. A miracle to behold. Laura Smith Biswas belongs to the second group. Her book, The Cosmology of Love, is the key to creating the right conditions for love.

So often, in matters of the heart, we find ourselves asking the wrong questions. We try to figure out what we're doing wrong, we ask ourselves if we are lovable, we wonder why love seems so elusive. We imagine ourselves bystanders, separate from love. The Cosmology of Love reunites us with love by asking all the right questions. How does the love we feel evolve into an expression of love that can be shared? How do we convey our love so the one we love feels loved? How do we, ourselves, receive love? The Cosmology of Love takes the reader through a process of discovery. A process that is alive and living. Laura Smith Biswas invites us beyond the conceptual into the practical as she skillfully guides the reader through more than 70 effective steps to recognizing, creating, building and sustaining relationships fueled with love.

Can you imagine what life would be if you had the ability to create love wherever you go? Who you would be if you were fluent in the language of love? I can't think of any better way to spend my time here on earth. I sense you probably feel the same. Enjoy the discoveries you'll make along the way.

Dawn Cartwright
Chandra Bindu Tantra Institute

CHAPTER 1

Introduction

Our motto at The Love Mandala is

Be Love

Why? Because we think that's the core essence of every person on the planet.

If we are made of love, then that gives us the opportunity to express it and be a force of love in the world. However, just because it is who we are at the core, doesn't mean we always know how to access it.

We can develop our ability to tap into love, align with it and learn to express our loving nature.

So that we experience profound love in our lives.

The foundation for being a more loving person lies in cultivating self-love.

We are blessed by starting with ourselves, as truly we are the only person we will relate to every moment of our lives. The way we hold ourselves, treat ourselves, talk to ourselves and prioritize our own needs or desires becomes a template for all our other interactions and relationships. As we learn to love ourselves, we tap into a powerful reservoir of loving to extend outwards. We cannot give far beyond what we have received in some measure.

Beyond this **foundation** we can explore how we relate with love to others. Are our choices, thoughts and actions loving? This can be a difficult question at times, because, for any given choice, it is possible to debate whether it was a loving choice. It can vary depending on an individual's perspective. However, our belief is that the **underlying intent** behind the choice or action is what defines it as loving. We cannot guarantee how it is received, but we can direct our choices with clear intent.

We can also explore with others how they wish to receive love and **Improve our ability to connect in loving relationships.** We all have preferences for how we like to give and receive love, which may even change over the course of time. Learning what those preferences are at any stage of life can help us communicate our love and open to more loving experiences all around.

One day I realized I was failing people I loved.

This book came from a moment of real frustration with my loved ones. I had been working very hard in a situation to convey my love, and I totally missed the mark. I felt disconnected and exasperated that despite my efforts things weren't working.

I realized that we can each value and communicate things uniquely, and I saw that within my family there were a myriad of possible approaches to expressing love. It was like realizing there was a whole universe of ways to give and receive love.

This led directly to the development of *The Cosmology of Love*. The intent of the book was clear for me. Create a tool to **identify specific ways of loving, inspire others to be more loving and stimulate discussion** between lovers and family members that could bring the experience of greater love into their relationships.

As the specific *Ways of Loving* were outlined that we could use in this work, it became clear that there were five key categories that they fell within:

- *Ways of Acting*
- *Ways of Being*
- *Ways of Speaking*
- *Ways of Thinking*
- *Ways of Touching*

While some of them may seem outrageously obvious, let me share a little bit of what each of these mean and provide some examples.

How to Use This Book

This book was written **to encourage, inspire, question and prompt** you as a reader to explore specific, detailed ways of loving yourself and then extending love into your other relationships.

In the *The Cosmology of Love* each page has **three** parts to present a specific Way of Loving.

1. A description of the *Way of Loving*.

2. Suggested key words that represent the underlying feelings that you may be seeking to experience behind the *Way of Loving*. These can be a simple guide to being more loving, as you hold the essence of the feeling in your focus.

3. Ideas and questions to explore how it can apply that way to your daily life.

Use the final section on p. 88 *Discovering Your Ways of Loving* to identify what is most important to you to feel loved. You can share this process with your loved ones so that you can understand their preferences more clearly for loving interactions. Share your top ways and enjoy the dialogue it stimulates to better connect and enjoy each other!

Use them also to cultivate how to care for yourself as well. For example, if you prefer *Word of Appreciation,* you can practice giving yourself positive verbal feedback in your self-talk.

Note: the companion book *Affirmations of Love: 400+ Affirmations to Create Profound Love* consists of an additional set of affirmations for each *Way of Loving* for those who want to reinforce the work in this way.

AS the specific Ways of Loving emerged in writing this book, it became clear that there were **5 key categories** that they fell within:

- *Ways of Acting*
- *Ways of Being*
- *Ways of Speaking*
- *Ways of Thinking*
- *Ways of Touching*

While some of them may seem outrageously obvious, let me share a little bit of what each of these mean and provide some examples.

Ways of Acting

Have you ever heard that love is a verb? Our visible actions of love are examples of that adage. We have so many choices that allow us to show love through outward action and generally people think of demonstrations of love most often in this way.

While there are so many actions of love to consider, I have found that the *Ways of Loving* that are most important to me in this category seem to be tied to those qualities I crave more of or had little of as a child.

Loving through an action can be expressed through a wide range of choices. A few of the loving *Ways of Acting* in this area include:

- Surprises / Unexpected Gifts
- Building Traditions
- Self-Responsibility / Accountability
- Creating Joy & Fun
- Acts of Service

Ways of Being

Loving interactions can also stem from the way we show up. I call this our *Way of Being*. When we present ourselves in the world, we can be expressing peace, respect, enthusiasm and a whole host of other attributes without even saying or doing anything. It is really how we are holding the moment inside that is our *Way of Being*. I grew up in a super busy house as the second of eight children. It was scarce to have moments of pure presence and quiet where I felt seen and heard. The ability of my loved ones to be present with me has become a highly valued Way of Loving in my life.

Our *Way of Being* can be expressed both in relationship to ourselves as well as in our interactions with others. Additionally, we can direct our love with our intent; for example, approaching a situation with a clear willingness to be vulnerable. Not only can we show up with a clear chosen focus like this, but we have the opportunity to ask and explore what qualities those we love are seeking, so that we can more powerfully relate to their needs and demonstrate our love.

Some other examples of how we can show love through our *Way of Being* include:

- Allowing Feelings
- Vulnerability
- Listening From the Heart
- Gentleness
- Compassion

Ways of Speaking

Our words are certainly one of the most obvious and powerful ways to express love. They can carry such power in moments such as saying, "I love you" to "I'm sorry." There are so many ways of expressing through words, from using song, face-to-face communication, leaving notes and sending texts, email and letters. Our ability to listen is also captured in this way of loving and there can be great love in communicating with our attention and questions to confirm our understanding while another speaks.

It is also of great value to connect soul to soul over ideas, dreams, stories and sharing feelings. These expressions can be deeply loving to exchange when coming from our authenticity.

Some of the *Ways of Speaking* that communicate love include:

- Words of Appreciation
- Sharing Laughter
- Words of Praise

- Asking for What You Want
- Sharing Feedback With Love

Ways of Thinking

Our thoughts have direct influence in how we open to ourselves and others in relationship. Whether it is shifting our thinking to being accepting or embracing the differences in another person, our thoughts have a powerful effect on how lovingly we approach the world.

Consciously observing how our thinking impacts our relationships can be a rich exploration to expanding our loving influence. Once we understand how we habitually respond in our thought process, we can turn our attention to redirecting our thinking as a tool and act of love. We can learn to open to new thought responses and exercise our capacity to cultivate more loving ones, opening the door to new opportunities and experiences of love.

Some examples of *Ways of Thinking* that can be lovingly cultivated are:

- Gratitude
- Non-Judgment
- Forgiveness
- Respecting Choices and Desires
- Curiosity

Ways of Touching

In all we do, our senses are some of the most powerful ways of relating as human beings. Touch can become a way of loving that ranges from comfort to ecstatic thrill. The value we put on pleasure and the senses plays into how important this is to us. Sometimes we forget how much a physical, tangible experience can offer when we have become used to a culture centered around the digital world or one with a heavy intellectual focus. Experimenting with what is most cherished through the body can be a joyful exploration in life.

As we explore touch as a means of loving, we can learn to engage our intentions or hearts in the process so that we are more present and focused in how we receive or give love through touch. It can change a small routine interaction into a magical experience and fill our lives with much more meaningful exchanges.

Some of the *Ways of Touching* that specifically connect us in love with others include:

- Cuddling
- Massage
- Sensuous Touch
- Caressing
- Kissing

You might play with these questions:

- What are the most powerful ways I desire to be loved?
- Is one *Way of Loving* more important to me than another?
- What can I do now I know my preferences, to offer myself more love?
- What can I communication to others, to enhance the experience of feeling loved and expressing more love?

These and many other *Ways of Touching*, *Thinking*, *Speaking*, *Being* and *Acting* are discussed in more detail within the book. I welcome you and honor your next step in the journey of cultivating greater love in your life and those around you.

My most fervent wish is for you to *experience* more profound love in your life.

CHAPTER 2

Ways of Acting

Accountability / Self-Responsibility

Our self-expression and happiness are greatly enhanced by recognizing that we are the authors of our lives. If we choose to think others are responsible for our experience, we handicap ourselves from our own creative power. If we see the daily choices we make are our responsibility then we can set the standard for our own care and steer our lives for the better. Oftentimes when we feel disappointed by others, it is a reflection that we need to nurture ourselves, establish boundaries, ask for what we want or clarify what we will accept. While we can't control others' behavior or many events in life, we do hold the responsibility to own our responses, perspectives, beliefs, actions and intentions.

Desired Feelings
Capable, Centered, Competent, Empowered, Responsible, Strong

What expectations have I laid on others that I could more fully own.

As I turn within seeking a change in my life, what part do I have influence over?

If others expect me to take care of their responsibilities, how do I hold firm that they are not mine to own?

Can I express confidence in my ability and the abilities of others to be the creators of our lives?

Does it feel more or less empowering to take ownership of this situation?

Do I need to take different actions to experience self responsibility?

Activating Joy & Fun

We all have a child within us that loves to play, and some souls have a natural ability to initiate joy and fun for others. This skill can be cultivated to spread happiness and demonstrate our love all around. For those of us who have had an austere upbringing, this might take practice and learning to take life less seriously and uncover our way of creating fun in life. It could show up as bringing enthusiasm to a situation, initiating a surprise or mischievous joke, physical play, teasing banter and much, much more.

As we cultivate our own happiness by meeting our needs for play, it is easier and easier to activate joy in others. Oftentimes, as adults we need to make a point of setting time aside from goals, work and responsibilities to create play time. As we do this, we can become a bright light and gift to others by sparking a new mood in a setting or spreading our inherent joy playfully.

Desired Feelings
Playful, Surprised, Entertaining, Joyful, Enthusiastic

What things did I love to do as a child that I have forgotten about?

Could I take things less seriously and see the humor in more situations?

What fun activities or playful choices could I bring to this day?What would be a way to bring fun into my work environment?Is there a surprise I could plan to delight another?

Have I invited life to bring more joy across my path?

Acts of Service

When I offer unexpected service, it allows me to show up in the world in a soft and generous way. Reaching out to assist another in need or make their life easier in some way is an outward demonstration of love. Extending myself to help someone in need, offer patience to a child or smile at a stranger, I contribute to making the world a more wonderful place. Service can cascade from one person to another as it is extended. Acts of service bring relief and support where someone may be experiencing difficulty. By showing genuine concern and asking how we can be of help, we open the door to new opportunities for grace in our lives.

Choosing to be of service without expectation can free us to know a beautiful part of ourselves regardless of how that service is received. We can also be of service to ourselves, by considering our own needs and responding to them without pushing them to the bottom of our list. It may pay to ask ourselves if we are stepping into an act of service from our own overflow or from a depleted, empty space. We may need to remember to provide care for ourselves first, before we can be of service to others from a state of abundance.

Desired Feelings
Generous, Open, Helpful, Supported, Charitable

How will being of service to me change how I relate to others?

If I met myself with an attitude of service, how could that affect my mood and day?

What opportunities for service will come my way today?

If I were to initiate an act of service in my home, how would it shift the feelings of those around me?

Is it possible a small act by me might snowball into more love or smiles in the world today?

Building Traditions

Building traditions or regular rituals that are personally meaningful can cultivate a sense of rhythm and create a more grounded or established way of living. Whether for an individual or family, the repetition of valued actions can be a supportive and loving expression of the heart. They allow us a means to celebrate and honor what is important to us.

Within families traditions can be cultivated across various races, cultures and religions to honor the underlying essence of what is cherished. They provide a means for making family memories and building markers along the passage of time. As an individual, ritual can also be a valuable part of self-care, establishing patterns of living that nurture and encourage joy in our lives.

Desired Feelings
Gentle, Soft, Lightness, Open-Hearted, Inclusive

 What family traditions bring me joy that I would want to continue?

Are there qualities in my partner's traditions that I love as well and can help them celebrate?

How could we blend our traditions into a unique celebration across the holidays?

Would a conversation be useful to discuss what we all want to do together to create happy memories?

What can we do to simplify our lives so we have greater presence and enjoyment during life celebrations?

What rituals would serve me to feel peaceful and centered in my life?

Cherishing Through Eye Gazing

If the eyes are the window to the soul, gazing fully into your own or the eyes of your loved ones is a gift of presence. Being seen and seeing others quietly without distraction and with love can profoundly move us all. Taking the time to connect through the eyes may be one of the most cherished actions we can offer. In many parts of our world, this act has become so infrequent it may feel too intimate to be comfortable at first. It may take courage to hold the gaze of another longer than you are used to, and doing it with an intention of love can shift us within powerfully.

A wonderful place to begin is to start with ourselves, as we see the essence of who we are beyond our bodies. When we pause to look into the eyes, cherishing the moment, it brings us fully into the present. A look that is not rushed can speak volumes of love and signal how much another means to us. It gives us a gift by allowing us to taste that moment fully, introducing more intimacy into our lives.

Desired Feelings
Present, Open, Intimate, Connected, Loving

Would looking myself in the mirror with love help me feel centered or connected?

Do I see myself with love and kindness when looking at my reflection?

Can I acknowledge the loving intent within me, as I gaze in the mirror?

What moments of the day might be welcome ones to turn into a more intimate exchange with my family?

Would eye gazing be a welcome way to start lovemaking with my partner?

Can I hold the gaze of strangers longer if only to introduce more presence into my life?

Creative Play

We all have a creative spirit that seeks nurturing and expression. Just as when we were children, our ability to get lost in play - creating something for no other reason than for the experience of it - seeks to emerge within us as adults. We might have resistance to this type of call, thinking we have little time for activities without a productive endpoint. However, there is a mystery to creative play. When we allow ourselves to tap into our creativity, we create freedom and generate new energy, ideas or inspirations that would otherwise not be found.

We may take a lesson from watching children create without judgment, get lost in the moment without worry and simply have fun for the sake of it. Doing this for ourselves is an act of self-care as we cultivate the innovative intelligence within you.

Desired Feelings
Expressive, Creative, Inspired, Present, Relaxed, Innovative

What creative actions would be fun for me today?

Am I willing to stop the train of productivity and pause for creative fun for 15 minutes today?

What benefits might I see if I stopped and took the time to nurture my creative impulse in some way?

Is there something my loved ones are asking me to do that is playful and not on my to-do list?

Are my five senses being nurtured and enjoyed in my creative activities?

Financial Support

Dedicating financial resources to myself or those I love can be a tangible act of love. As I receive the resources I need monetarily, I allow for my fullest expression to come forward in life. As I contribute financially to others, I provide a tangible gift to fuel their path as they see fit, honoring their choices. Whether a small gift or large one, the flow of money exchanged with gratitude fuels more abundance in one's life.

Our ability to talk openly about our needs is a powerful first step in exploring means of support. If we are on the other side, as we share monetary support freely for the blessing of all it fosters an open flow of resources. Seeing the love behind the exchange makes it all the sweeter, and allows one to feel the support that our divine inheritance offers in life. As an individual we may find that trusting that we can create the financial support for our dreams and goals is the ingredient we need. Our choice to believe in our capacity to create wealth is the first step in opening up to the various ways it can come about.

Desired Feelings
Resourceful, Gracious, Abundant, Receptive, Overflowing

Where could I show gratitude for what I already have received?

How would I show up in the world if I was abundantly supported to live out my purpose?

Where have I been uncomfortable receiving in my life?

Have I learned to trust the exchange of resources in my home, respecting the differences in expression?

Where could I more freely share what I have been blessed with and contribute to the financial support of those around me?

How could I help my children develop their own capacity to create financial strength?

Kindness

Acts of kindness towards myself and others provide a gentle interaction that softens the heart and allows me to open and relax. Loving words, choices and expressions of allowance are signs of kindness. Allowance might look like giving others the room to be themselves without comment or judgment. Kindness is also often visible. It may show up as unexpected aid, where one is struggling physically. A kind heart may be revealed through the act of forgiveness or through gentle words of encouragement. Opening to the idea that we do not always know the full story of another may allow us to engage as a more kind person.

As we are kind to ourselves, we have greater capacity to share this same trait with others. We can cultivate the ability to be easy, nonjudgmental or soft in our inner dialogue with ourselves daily. Generosity is a sign of kindness. Another helpful tool is choosing to see all people as worthy no matter what. It opens the door to giving and receiving acts of kindness without condition.

Desired Feelings
Gentle, Soft, Open-hearted, Light, Generous

 Where could I show gratitude for what I already have received?

How would I show up in the world if I was abundantly supported to live out my purpose?

Where have I been uncomfortable receiving in my life?

Have I learned to trust the exchange of resources in my home, respecting the differences in expression?

Where could I more freely share what I have been blessed with and contribute to the financial support of those around me?

How could I help my children develop their own capacity to create financial strength?

Physical Care & Nurturance

Our relationship to our bodies is a foundational area of self-love. Our physical form seeks to support us in our life purpose, offering joy and the means to fulfill our dreams. As the embodiment of our Spirit, providing physical care is an expression of love for the whole person. Working with our individual needs for physical movement, nourishing foods, sleep, rest and play are all areas to explore what serves us to best. These choices help us to show up in the world in a most loving way. The heartfelt intentions underlying our choices guide how effectively we nurture ourselves and others.

Developing consistency in caring for ourselves is a paramount act of love. As our responsibilities increase as adults, we are often challenged to learn to prioritize care for ourselves. We can benefit from recognizing the difference in how we show up when our own needs are satisfied vs. when they are not. Boundaries that establish time for ourselves as parents for example, can be the key factor in allowing us to show up with more love all around. We might find that observing our mix of work, play and rest can help us calibrate a nurturing balance over time.

Desired Feelings
Healthy, At Ease, Supported, Nourished, Balanced

What do I need right now physically to feel balanced - a break, rest or some play?

What areas of self-care do I choose daily that I can appreciate? What am I modeling to my children?

What thoughts can bring my body into relaxed and vibrant health?

What is an easy step to establish solid physical self-care?

What do I need so I can show up with love and energy in my life?

Am I establishing boundaries to create space in my life?

Where can I add more support to myself to support my dreams?

Sharing in Activities

We all have things we like to do in the world that feed our souls and bring fun or inspiration to our lives. When we engage in an activity that we or our loved ones enjoy, we send the message that we value that desire. Either way, we provide an opportunity to explore who we are, create a memory together or simply do something for no other reason than to enjoy one another.

Our full attention and engagement in the activity pulls us into the joy of the present moment. It may provide opportunities for bonding or conversation that would otherwise not happen. When we choose to engage in an activity just for our own satisfaction, we nourish our self-worth, signaling that we are just as important as anyone else in our lives. We choose inclusion rather than leaving ourselves behind in trying to assist everyone else.

Desired Feelings
Interested, Open, Engaged, Collaborative, Present, Connected

What is one thing I've always wanted to do but have put off?

Can I choose to take 10 or 15 minutes to do something I love to do that isn't on my task list?

What can I enjoy with my family that will show I value what they care about?

If I were to jump into this activity, trusting it would strengthen our relationship, what would that look like?

Could a one-on-one activity benefit our connection and feeling of closeness?

Supporting Learning & Growth

My development or growth as an individual seeks to continue throughout my life. As I acknowledge this part of me or support others to do the same, I feed the soul's desire to evolve and expand. This choice sustains relationships over the long run as it allows each to grow into their potential and transform. When we support our own or another's need to take a class or develop a new skill, or when we offer financial or other tangible support, we demonstrate a caring that is beyond our own benefit. It extends to contributing to the expression of the whole person regardless of our understanding of the why's behind the desire.

When we move beyond the basic needs being met, personal growth is a significant desire that is expressed. In honoring it, we see the blossoming of the individual over time. Supporting growth over the long term within ourselves or as a parent may require sustained focus, resources and effort. Regardless of the investment, it shows deep love to make that commitment and to believe in the capacity and potential of us all.

Desired Feelings
Stimulated, Expansive, Evolving, Maturing, Whole

Have I made time for myself to develop my skills, talents or interests even when I don't know why they call to me?

Can I carve out 15 minutes a day to practice what I desire to develop within myself?

What is the passion I see in those around me that calls to be expressed and supported?

What words or actions would support my loved ones in their evolution and expression to be all they can be?

Surprises / Unexpected Gifts

The joy of the unanticipated can be a creative way to express love and to enjoy engaging with others. Spontaneity brings spice and a freshness to our interactions that can demonstrate loving attention. We can both create surprises for others as well as choose spontaneity for ourselves. The latter might be done by offering our inner child a time each week to do something out of the ordinary in our routine, just for fun. Giving ourselves a gift, perhaps of fresh flowers, a new book, time off to play a game, can all signal self-love and nourish the playful side of us.

The uniqueness of a surprise or gift that is not anticipated may signal to another that we have been thinking of them beyond the daily routine. It signals our appreciation and indicates how we hold them precious in our lives. The soul may crave variety and newness in our daily life and this is a fun way to introduce it. The satisfaction of creating such an interaction for another can also be a rewarding feeling to relish.

Desired Feelings
Spontaneity, Joy, Fun, Playful, Generous

What could I do to nourish the gift of spontaneity in my life?

If I took 10 minutes today to gift myself with something new, what would I choose to do?

Looking inside, what would my inner child ask for?

Have I made the time to plan ahead for special occasions to create something meaningful with my loved ones?

If I let my creativity out, what would it say about adding fun and joy to my relationships?

Could I leave a note or small token of love for another that would make their day?

CHAPTER 3

Ways of Being

Accepting All of Me

Relating to ourselves and others in wholeness is a choice to embrace the fullness of who we are without conditions. Being embraced fully allows us to feel encased in love and to experience feeling safe and secure. Relating in wholeness is demonstrated by choosing to love a part of us that we initially see as 'less than' or loving another for their differences, without exception. These choices demonstrate unconditional love for all aspects of the whole.

We may find that these parts are not always easily understood, but denying them fractures the sense of self and cuts us and others off from learning fully who we are. These parts of ourselves can be tremendous teachers to us or a pathway to healing. Embracing honestly what is present within us or others without judgment, allows for growth and transformation.

Desired Feelings
Allowing, Peaceful, Whole, Embraced

What parts of myself have I neglected looking at?

What areas of my life have I considered problematic because I am unlike my family or peers?

If I were to actually embrace those parts, what benefits would be available to me?

How could I extend myself to embrace all the aspects of those I love?

What would it mean to them if I was willing to do that?

Am I willing to drop the perception of being 'right' in exchange for acceptance?

Acknowledging / Allowing Feelings

We are not our feelings, and yet they are so powerful at times we can get lost in them. In taking care of ourselves, we can learn to experience our feelings with acceptance rather than avoiding or over identifying with them. Our health is in part dependent on whether we can allow ourselves to shift and flow energetically with them. Avoiding unpleasant feelings or suppressing them creates a heaviness and calls for them to intensify being heard. While it is human to avoid pain, the easier path is to create a relationship of allowing and acknowledging our feelings.. We may need to be quiet, take a walk or meditate to create the space to acknowledge them. We can also simply let them be felt, trusting they will shift. When facing particularly difficult or persistent feelings, we may benefit from giving them voice out loud or on paper to learn about ourselves and release them.

It is empowering to realize our feelings are significantly influenced by how we think about the experiences we have day to day. Our perspective is the filter that leads us ultimately to the feelings that rise within us. We have choices in every thought that can lead us to a lighter or heavier feeling. It can take practice to cultivate thinking that leads to positive feeling states. We may find that uplifting feelings are actually not that familiar and we need to stretch into letting them last longer and encouraging them to stick around.

Desired Feelings
Heard, Peaceful, Honest, Integrated, Reflective

What feelings am I most comfortable with and which ones do I avoid? Is there a creative way to express them?

How can I create a more welcoming place for all I feel?

What intention could I set to experience feelings with more grace?

Would I benefit from tracking how my thoughts lead to different feelings?

Can I allow myself to feel good longer and stay open with more positivity?

Allowing Space or Time Alone

We all need time in our lives regularly where we are alone to just be or do as we please. Sometimes when we bump up against a difficult challenge inside or with another, it is the hardest time but perhaps the most valuable time to allow space. There is a spectrum of how much time we each need to recharge and create peace with ourselves. Communicating and respecting the need for space can go a long way towards building a healthy foundation between us all in daily living.

We may need to give ourselves permission and/or discuss it openly with others to find harmony in creating the time or space we need. Freely extending time and quiet to our loved ones as they need is a sign of love and respect. If we can honestly assess our own needs and take daily steps to provide the time or space we need, we are likely to find it sustaining and supportive of us being our best selves. It allows us to give more freely as we are coming from a place of support. As we trust others to take what they need, we may find them return to us with greater openness and appreciation.

Desired Feelings
At Ease, Spacious, Free, Centered, Calm

What small step could I take today to give myself room to relax and be nourished?

What can I do to give space to myself or loved one when we have had a conflict or busy day?

How would taking time for either one of us to be alone provide more capacity to meet in a loving space together?

Is there a need in our home to create more down time for contemplation, imagination, rest and relaxation?

Do I feel peaceful within or rushed and overwhelmed? Can I allow myself a few minutes of peace to recharge today whenever I need it?

Attentiveness

We cannot experience love without attention. On a certain level, attention is the common thread in all ways of loving - without a focus we have nothing and with it we can shape our experience. We may see this skill as learning to combine presence with intention. When we show up fully in the moment and with a focused intent to be loving, we become a force of love either to ourselves or others. We can harness our attention to offer support, love, share from our heart, listen, witness or comfort.

Giving ourselves loving attention is a fundamental skill of self-care. When we rush past our needs, ignore our feelings or deprioritize ourselves in our lives, we suffer. When we seek to bring what is important to us to the surface, risk acting on our dreams, or place ourselves in the equation of our families to get our own needs met, then we build a foundation of strength. We are saying, "I am important in my own life." When we provide attention to another, we send the strong message, "You are important to me and I love you."

Desired Feelings
Present, Open, Focused, Heard, Loving

What areas of my life are popping up for attention regularly?

When I need support, do I give myself permission to receive it?

What might that support be?

How can I slow down to see what needs attention in my life and my family's life?

What would it look like to offer attention for myself when difficult emotions arise?

How could I be more present in love in the small moments?

Being Present

Oftentimes, life is calling for our full attention to be focused in the moment, whether it is for ourselves or another person. Stopping what we are doing to turn within is powerful and can be a profound act of love. Modern life is full of activity, striving and to-do lists for most people. We often crave simple presence, attention and focus. When we are hurting, confused, doubtful, afraid or angry or grieving, the self is calling for attention. We can choose to be fully present when we are suffering in any way by listening or holding a focus of compassion. This is a tremendous gift.

With others, when we are willing to give them our full attention, we signal their importance in our life and allow their needs to be expressed and heard. It has been said that all attention is love. Fully offering that attention in an undivided way to others communicates our love. This way of being allows us to surrender to what is present in our lives and calling for our focus, despite all the grand plans we had for our day.

Desired Feelings
Calm, Peaceful, Aware, Relaxed, Attentive

Where have I ignored myself and a call to stillness?

Can I cultivate a sense of listening to myself to witness what is arising inside?

What is unheard in my heart that is speaking to me?

Do I stop what I am doing with my family to give them full attention at key points throughout our time together?

Can we cultivate a family practice of time together without distractions?

Can I experiment with trusting the flow of life, rather than watching the clock?

Boundaries

One of the most loving gifts to ourselves is establishing boundaries that support us and allow us to be our best selves. We can apply this both to how we relate with ourselves as well as others. Just like children, we all need parameters or structure so we can function well. When we are growing up, this falls to our parents to establish, but as we mature, we learn that it is our responsibility to set and maintain them. Our ability to become aware of what truly supports us, communicate this to others and follow our own wisdom, provides a consistent foundation for our well-being.

Our boundaries may show up as physical or space requirements for sleep, rest, time to be alone or to do the things that recharge us. They may also look like saying no to over committing or people pleasing, communicating when an arrangement is no longer working for us, or even dropping out of conversations or situations that feel draining to us. It may also be setting boundaries in areas such as physical touch or money. One key to recognize is that when we have our boundaries clearly in place and share them with others, it provides our own support so that we can show up for others in a much more loving way. We are free to set and revise them. We are empowered by knowing that they are a gift even when others object, because it ultimately creates more loving interactions for all involved.

Desired Feelings
Whole, Clear, Supported, Balanced, Safe

 Do I realize I have the power and responsibility to set my own boundaries?

Where have I failed to communicate my boundaries?

How would my loved ones benefit from me getting the sleep, space and support I need?

Where is one place that I can communicate what I need that would give me relief and empower me?

Would our family benefit from a conversation about boundaries and how they help us? Are they clear?

Cultivating Trust

Trust comes from being comfortable on a deeper level with the journey of life. When we lack trust, it is typically rooted in fear, so offering trust is essentially voting in favor of the core essence of love that exists within all of us. Cultivating trust with ourselves is the fundamental work we must do to be able to offer it to others. We build trust through consistency in our verbal agreements and actions. Agreements may at times need revision and we can benefit from looking at whether they need adjustment when we experience a gap. Looking at where we lack trust in our own selves or in life is also a worthwhile exercise when we struggle with it.

We extend trust to others, by giving them room to act freely without manipulation or control. It may require us to step back and trust the flow of life on a grander scale even when it feels scary. If others break our trust, we can benefit from exploring competing intentions, unspoken expectations or developing maturity. Holding authentic conversation about our feelings through the process, applying forgiveness and exploring what would work better, can help us move through issues of trust.

Desired Feelings
Alignment, Whole, Peace, Allowing, Grace

Do I trust myself to come from a place of love? Do I trust my desires are guiding me for the highest good?

Do I act in a trustworthy manner with my loved ones? Do I keep my commitments or revise them openly as needed?

Am I choosing to give those I love room to build trust with me?

Can I openly discuss what my wishes are with my loved ones?

Are there instances where I have been given an opportunity to rebuild trust and can I offer that to others?

Is there sufficient trust as a foundation to build intimacy?

Elevating Your Feeling State

We all have the capacity to care for ourselves by working with our own feelings to care for and enhance them. It is a highly valuable skill to learn to enhance our feeling state as it affects not just us but all those around us. We can learn to be great stewards of our emotions. When we pay attention to them, take responsibility for them and realize that we can cultivate increasingly better ones, we find our power. This is the power to craft our lives and experience shifts from the inside out. So many people have not been taught to cultivate their feelings and have been left to temporary, ineffective solutions. While there is nothing to judge in this, we can find relief and joy in life by cultivating this skill from within.

One approach to cultivating a good feeling state is to explore what actions, beliefs and thoughts support lighter, more uplifting feelings. By daily observation, we can begin to see what truly supports our happiness and what detracts from it that we can control. An approach that may help is to have a toolbox of 'go-to' solutions when we don't feel good. It might be a list such as: positive friends to call, a feel good movie or comedy segment waiting to be seen, a physical activity, a practice of writing or meditation. Whatever works is a blessing and can be embraced. We may find that as we cultivate better feelings, we learn to amplify and enhance them, creating more joy in our lives.

Desired Feelings
Powerful, Energized, Happy, Light, Resourceful

What do I know about my patterns that influence my mood?

How can I ease into the morning so that I feeling better throughout the day?

What are my favorite ways to feel better that are healthy for me?

How do I affect those around me with my energy?

Can I see how to turn the tables on my feelings by interrupting them with a feel-good action?

Gentleness

The quality of gentleness while associated with the feminine, can be shared by men and women equally and is a powerful demonstration of love. Especially if we were not treated with gentleness as a child, learning to let go of responding to the world with hardness and leading with a softer approach is a significant shift towards love. Gentleness can be expressed in our tone, selection of words, actions and even how we feel when we approach others. Starting with ourselves and checking on how we relate to ourselves when we struggle is a great place to start.

As we learn to be gentle with ourselves through daily challenges, we then find it easier to offer it to others. It may consist of reaching for a feeling of compassion when we are upset rather than judging our response. It could be speaking a kind word of encouragement when we feel we have made a mistake. We might invite gentleness by focusing on softening the feeling around our hearts or checking on whether we feel open and unguarded. This reminds us to relate with softness to ourselves and others.

Desired Feelings
Soft, Open, Tender, Kind

Where could I soften my approach with myself and others?

Where would bringing gentleness add volumes of love in my life?

Can I recognize that I did not learn how to be gentle with myself and start now as a beginner?

How do I want others to feel when I approach them?

What is a word or act of gentleness that I could bring to myself or family today?

Holding My Center In Love

We all face moments in our lives where we experience discord with another, and we can bring love to ourselves and others as we hold our center. Placing our focus in our hearts and holding a broader perspective of what is unfolding can aid us all greatly.

If we have adopted a people-pleasing orientation, we may need to relearn what it means to allow others to have their feelings without taking them in and adopting them. It can take practice to be compassionate with others, while not getting lost in their view.

What might it mean to hold in love and stay centered in the face of upset? We can focus on acknowledging feelings, without turning it into a judgment of right and wrong. If we feel triggered with difficult emotions, we can step away and focus on loving ourselves to come back to center. In some situations, reminding ourselves of our original intent prior to a misunderstanding can help us hold ourselves in innocence. We can bless others during times of difficulty, by holding a loving focus in our minds. We might envision that the child within them is hurting and recognize there is a higher truth beyond the hurt. If we maintain our balance, we are able to hold positive intent for others as they work through their struggles.

Desired Feelings
Peace, Understanding, Solace, Harmony, Balanced

What way could I see the person in front of me that would disentangle me from arguing and support more understanding?

Do I desert myself easily when others are upset with me?

Do I avoid conflicts because I am still learning to hold my center?

If I could hold one thought of peace during an argument, what would that be?

Would another benefit from me remembering that they will come through this difficulty and return to peace?

Can I focus on the love I have during this challenging discussion?

Holding Space for Others

We all need support and a listening ear at times, and having someone intentionally hold space for us allows us to move through our challenges more gracefully. Holding space for another is akin to placing an anchor beneath them to provide stability in a storm. We might not understand how it works, but simply focusing on the strength, capability and divine potential of another can assist them to see it within. We can do this as we listen to others, maintaining a positive vision of their inherent ability to ultimately overcome all things in their lives.

It can be a blessing to simply be sitting with another who believes in us and maintains a positive focus for us to overcome our pain, grief or fear despite how dark it looks in the moment. This way of being can provide energetic support whether we are physically near or far from someone we love who is struggling.

Desired Feelings
Confident, Steady, Solace, Supportive, Compassionate

How does my attitude affect those around me as they work through their life's material?

Can I hold a positive focus for myself when I'm in pain and imagine coming through this challenge?

Can I embody confidence as I sit with another who is struggling?

How do I open to holding positive thoughts for others in their growth?

What focus could I provide in this moment that offers strength and courage?

I Am Love

Our inherent nature is divinely loving. We come from the essence of love, cannot separate ourselves from it and have the opportunity to emanate it in all we do. Every chance we have to demonstrate this is a movement towards our true nature. We do this by deeply cultivating a loving attitude towards ourselves, our actions, thoughts and feelings. We can at times certainly act in ways that are childish, choose judgment, overreact to others and temporarily forget we are love. However, we are free in every moment to choose over and over to return to the wellspring of love within us.

This might look like a wide range of behaviors. For example, it could be deciding to accept ourselves as is, choosing to see how the universal desire for love is behind a wide range of behaviors, holding ourselves as innocent when we falter, or pausing to ask what is the most loving way to respond to a difficult situation. It may help to be aware that every step that we take is part of the assured journey to return to love. Whether it is a lesson in something we wish to do differently or a joyful experience where we discovered how to be more loving, it guides us back home. This awareness brings softness and light to our lives, which we can then extend to others.

Desired Feelings
Centered, Rooted in Love, Expansive, Emanating Love, Present

Can I embrace my actions, thoughts or feelings with love?

Can I hold myself or others innocent and in a learning process?

Do I see the divine essence of love within myself or others in this moment?

Where am I holding places of judgment or resentment that hold me back from more love?

What would love guide me do today? Where have I held myself hostage for in the past so I can now let go?

Listening From the Heart

One of the most profound ways to open the doorway to feeling and sharing love is to listen with great presence. Listening from the heart is done without the need to fix or repair any perceived problems. When we listen to ourselves or someone listens to us in this way, it offers respect for one's ability to meet life's challenges. It presents an opportunity for each of us to see we have all the resources inside to find our way forward.

Listening from the heart can be cultivated by focusing one's awareness on the heart, listening beyond the speaker's words and being fully present in the moment. It is the practice of bringing pure awareness and acceptance to what is happening in the moment and extending compassion. The offering of one's full attention allows the speaker to feel held in love and provides space to work through a solution from the inner wisdom within. Listening from the heart may require some practice to shift one's focus away from thinking, solving and responding, but both parties may find it is more moving and helpful in the end.

Desired Feelings
Understanding, Present, Aware, Supportive, Loving

What if I was free to listen without feeling the need to fix anything?

What if all I needed to do was be fully here and offer my heart and a listening ear?

What if in listening to myself I found great solace and comfort inside?

How can I stay present with those I love when I listen to them?

What helps me move into my heart instead of the mind?

Can I suspend thinking about my response while listening?

Can I hold a compassionate focus throughout?

Patience

While the quality of patience may be more naturally evident in some people, we can all cultivate it with our intentions and choices. When we look at how much patience we offer ourselves in our own process, it is a parallel that is reflected out to others. At times, we may benefit from accepting that we don't know how long it will take for us or others to learn something. We may find some areas of life that are quick to change and others that we work with for long periods of our lives. The same goes for other people. Reminding ourselves of this variation and not expecting progress on a preset timeline can be a compassionate way to relate with love. In addition, we learn that in the heat of frustration, patience is like an oasis in the desert. It eases our pain and allows us to begin again.

Desired Feelings
Allowing, Encouraging, Accepting, Peaceful, Compassionate

What is the form of patience I can offer myself today that would give me relief or a feeling of grace?

Can I let go of the timeline I had in my head for when I thought I would achieve something or overcome a challenge?

What intention or action could I offer to my loved ones to encourage them in their frustration?

Would patience with myself demonstrate to others that acceptance is more powerful than force?

Will patience enable me to return to peace and the flow of life?

Recognizing My Inherent Worth

Our inherent worthiness is a little talked about concept. The idea that we are worthy for no reason at all, simply through our existence, may be a new idea. We may think we need to do something to "earn" worthiness. We often grow up with a sense that we must be good, or that we must achieve or perform in some conditional way to feel worthy. This is a great misconception that limits our ability to access our internal lovability. We not only need not earn it, but nothing we can do can change it. No experience, mistake or weakness can negate the value of a soul. We can view our lives as a collection of experiences that cannot change our value no matter whether we see them as positive or negative.

Recognizing our worth can also be a tool for opening ourselves to fulfillment of our dreams, allowing us to drop any conditions that we may have thought needed to be met for us to pursue them. As we tap into the truth that our value cannot be questioned, we can more easily see that no person is more or less worthy than another. It supports us to perceive all people on a level playing field, seeing each person as important in their own right.

Desired Feelings
Appreciated, Unquestioned, Valued, Treasured, Embraced

Do I have a sense of feeling worthy? What does worthy feel like?

Do I limit myself in believing what I 'deserve' or can receive in life?

What is the next step in opening to feeling worthy?

Do I offer unconditional love to myself and others?

What would it mean to see all people as worthy as I went about my day?

When I feel I have misstepped, can I tap into my value being unchanged?

Self-Awareness

Developing self-awareness is a commitment to our soul's evolution. It means we are willing to pay attention to how we interact and show up in the world for better or for worse. It is the choice to observe ourselves and take responsibility for who we are in both the light and darkness. Learning to approach ourselves with loving kindness allows us to be more self-aware as we drop the expectation of perfection, and we can see our imperfection with love, humor and patience.

Being self-aware ultimately leads us to move beyond limiting patterns and beliefs. As we observe how we criticize, judge, limit or hold ourselves back in life, we naturally seek the means to grow and release ourselves from these behaviors. We are also more able to be honest with others when we make mistakes, owning and taking responsibility for our behavior. Self-awareness is the willingness to honestly assess ourselves and acknowledge both the shadow and light within us.

Desired Feelings
Embraced, Seen, Authentic, Clear, Accepting

What does self-awareness mean in my life?

Do I observe myself and patterns on a daily basis?

What do I wish to change?

Can I admit when I make a mistake and take responsibility for it?

Can I own my positive aspects and gracefully accept compliments?

Can I be lovingly aware of all aspects of me whether I see them as positive or negative?

Showing Compassion

Compassion is a form of love where we step into another's shoes and allow our hearts to be filled with empathy for their position. It requires us to suspend judgment to provide compassion for ourselves. As we practice it within, we are more easily able to access it as a quality as we relate to others. The essence of compassion comes from an assumption that it is not our place to judge or at the very least not helpful.

When we focus on the human experience in the moment, rather than the story behind the pain, we more easily open to compassion. It stems from letting go of trying to understand the why and moving straight into applying kindness, gentleness and love to an individual who is hurting. Compassion is simply about applying a balm to a wound, nothing else.

Desired Feelings
Open-hearted, Comforted, Consoled, Gentle

When I am hurting, can I offer compassion to myself just like I do to others?

What would it look like to be compassionate in this situation?

Can I let go of my preset ideas of why pain is present and move into offering comfort?

Am I letting others' judgments affect how I am reacting to this situation?

What if I was in this position, how would I want others to approach me?

Surrender

Surrender is the choice to let go of our predisposed ideas, expectations and the desire to control life so that we may allow what is present to be for the moment. It is a way of being where we relinquish control and shift into being open to what is occurring in our lives. It is a way of loving ourselves as it removes us from the internal resistance we create in life. It can also be loving to others as it enables us to disengage when in conflict or desire to change another.

Surrender provides a magical opportunity for us when we step into this way of relating. It opens the door to let go of our chosen position and crack the mind to what might be trying to emerge in our lives despite our best laid plans. It asks us to acknowledge that there is a larger perspective that we may not understand and seek to be open, curious and accepting of what is emerging. It may require us to grieve to let go of our picture of life, but shifting into surrender brings relief, comfort and greater flow.

Desired Feelings
Allowance, Relief, Alignment, Open, Non-Attachment

When I am fighting against what is, can I choose to let go?

What would surrender call me to do in this moment?

Can I let go of how I want things to go and allow life to unfold?

What do I need to trust in to surrender my need for control?

What feelings might shift if I surrendered myself to what is present in my life?

Would yoga, walking, meditation or some other calming practice help me to release my attachment and pain?

Can I remember I am unconditionally loved as I accept what is present in my life?

Vulnerability

Allowing ourselves to be vulnerable takes great courage. It is trusting that your openness and truth is more powerful than holding back or putting on a front of perfectionism to get an outcome you want. Vulnerability is opening ourselves up, taking a step forward to risk being seen in a new way, or perhaps showing our emotions and sharing our thoughts in a way where we feel exposed but truly honest.

When we believe we need to be perfect or hide our weaknesses from others to be loved, we hinder our ability to be authentic and extend vulnerability. Learning to trust that connection is built on truth enables us to step forward into a new way of relating with others. Transparency in our relationships with others opens the door to a new range of possibilities as new information is shared, connection encouraged and trust extended. As we take care of our own emotional needs and learn to love ourselves unconditionally, it empowers us to engage with others in a vulnerable, authentic and powerful way. Vulnerability may not be comfortable as we step into it, but it brings the alchemy of transformation to our lives.

Desired Feelings
Authentic, Clear, Open, Heartfelt, Connected

What if it was safe to be vulnerable?

How would it affect my relationships if I trusted opening up more authentically with others?

Could I be hiding my true feelings to feel safe?

What might help me drop the armor of protection and step up first to share more authentically?

What would a vulnerable statement look like in this

situation?

Am I willing to see vulnerability as a strength now?

Wholeness

Wholeness is the embracing of all our parts without diminishing or separating them. It can also be understood as recognizing that despite our human experience, we are fundamentally unbroken. In fact, we can view the experience of healing as likened to returning to the truth of our wholeness rather than a 'fixing' of it. It is divinely loving to hold every aspect of ourselves in the embrace of love. This might look like holding the viewpoint that even when different parts of us are confusing or trouble us, there is an underlying need for them to be cared for and welcomed home.

An example of this could be recognizing that a part of us that seeks to control situations is an effort to simply try to keep us safe. We can work with an aspect like this with a simple intention to bring this part in harmony with our other desires and remind ourselves that we are safe in this moment, no matter what has happened in the past. We can use our imagination to dialogue with aspects, even personalizing them to show compassion, ask for cooperation and reassign them to support us in a new way. Another way to experience our wholeness might be to hold our past in loving kindness, realizing that when we have made 'mistakes' we did so as part of a journey of discovering the truth of who we are, and not with malicious intent. A self-forgiving attitude calls each part of us home with a warm, gentle welcome.

Desired Feelings
Complete, Satisfied, Worthy, Integrated, Embraced

Are there parts of myself that might feel splintered off?

How can I forgive myself so that I can embrace all of me?

How would I feel if I valued every aspect of myself and invited each one home? Could I see myself as whole regardless of how others feel?

Are there any aspects of me that reflect a child seeking compassion and comfort?

Would I feel more integrated if I accepted what I perceive as my weaknesses?

CHAPTER 4

Ways of Speaking

Apologizing

We are all responsible for our own feelings. No one can force anyone to feel a certain way. However, that does not mean we can't apologize when another is hurt, even inadvertently. We might have acted poorly in retrospect or been surprised by another's feelings after an interaction that was well-intentioned. We all have things to learn, and respecting another's feelings is fundamental to building intimacy.

Saying I'm sorry verbally and expressing our empathy is a significant act of love. When genuinely offered, it can open the door to healing and peace. While we cannot predict another's readiness to receive our apology, we can offer it with love and be open to new conversations of what is really wanted in our interactions. This stands true as we relate to ourselves as well. Sometimes acknowledging to ourselves how sorry we are for the hurt inside is just what is needed to heal.

Desired Feelings
Peace, Respect, Honor, Acceptance, Acknowledged, Responsible

Are there any hurts inside that are asking for compassion?

Where have I been defensive with others? Would it be beneficial to drop my guard and apologize?

Could I show compassion for the feelings of another without making myself feel wrong?

Am I free and honest with the words, "I'm sorry?" What would a heartfelt apology feel like?

Do I over use "sorry," apologizing for things that are not my responsibility?

Can I share with another that I have been hurt to open the door to healing?

Do I need to take time to be with my own pain inside and then look at what feels best to do?

Asking For What You Want

Speaking our truth about our needs, wishes or desires is essential to creating truly loving relationships. Having the clarity and courage to communicate allows us to be met more completely as a whole person. We might have fears or pre-judgments about what others will think, say or feel in return, but our ability to create a life fully expressing ourselves is only possible when we allow our truth to shine forth.

This choice establishes a foundation of self-love, honoring our truth and demonstrating how we take responsibility for ourselves. If this is a new skill, it may be easiest to start with communicating small desires without attachment to outcome, to simply feel the strength that comes from expressing authentically. In addition, we may find that we need to clear a perception or fear of selfishness when we are actually only including ourselves in the picture to be understood. When everyone expresses their wishes or needs and others equally respond from their truth and authenticity, it allows all to be met more fully without manipulation.

Desired Feelings
Clear, Understood, Seen, Valued, Authentic, Transparent

In what areas of my life have I held back expressing myself?

In what areas do I find ease doing this?

When I am asked what I want, how honest am I?

Do I feel free to be myself in all situations and ask for what I need?

What could I say to others to help them feel at ease in communicating their true desires or needs?

What enables authentic communication in my life?

How do I model this skill to my children?

Authentic, Honest Communication

What keeps us from authenticity is often fear. Loving ourselves is the first step to being honest with others. As we practice speaking the truth in small things, we learn to trust being ourselves in the world and speaking up in significant matters with others. We learn that there is a link between being authentic and cultivating intimacy and connection.

We might find that we need to first work with ourselves to find our truth in a situation before speaking it. Other times we may know it, but be challenged to share it courageously or need to explore the most loving way to express it. Honest communication does not mean necessarily that we have no private part of our lives. Intimacy is not cultivated from knowing every last detail or fact. It is more powerfully nurtured by sharing what we feel and experience. We can follow our own inner wisdom of what is best to share in any given situation from a place of love.

Desired Feelings
At Ease, Honest, Transparent, Integrated, Connected

What is the essence within me that seeks to be spoken?

What is the truth of how I feel about this? What words are the closest reflection of those feelings?

When I acknowledge my feelings, do I feel safe to share them?

Have I welcomed my partner's or children's feelings and thoughts with openness?

Am I ready to accept differences in how I or others feel, without judging what it may mean?

Am I sharing what is truly important and honest in my communication?

Do I trust my intuition when it tells me there is more than what I am hearing?

Communicating During Conflict

While it is inevitable that we have differences and experience conflict with those we love, we have choices in how to communicate about them. For some, having courage to speak up is the challenge, while for others, learning to share feelings with diplomacy is an opportunity. In both cases it is beneficial to start with owning your own reactions and feelings regardless of what another has done. A great first step is allowing your feelings to simply be acknowledged and felt in the body.

Sharing them without blame provides a window for both parties to be open to understanding, healing and finding solutions that are mutually agreeable. Being willing to talk about feelings, even when there is concern that another won't want to hear them, provides the gift of allowing the other to understand your inner experience. When a partner who is more reactive and verbal in the moment of upset takes time to cool down before sharing their feelings, they increase the sense of safety for the conversation. Going on a walk or writing out our anger to clear the initial intensity of emotions in preparation to talk opens the door to a calmer exchange of feelings. This naturally allows for greater intimacy and connection in the long run.

Desired Feelings
Authentic, Balanced, Open, Cooperative, Trusting

Do I honor my feelings and allow them to be heard?

Can I meet myself with compassion and gentleness?

Am I withholding my true feelings or harboring resentments?

Do I take the time to nurture my own wounds?

Would it help me to work out or write out my pain and anger before expressing?

Would our family benefit from having a discussion about handling conflict and what it could look like?

Do I allow others to fully express their feelings, knowing they are valid even if I do not understand their reaction?

Reflective Listening

Reflective listening is a tremendous gift to everyone involved in conversation. It is not merely repeating what the speaker has said but using our intuition, curiosity and attention to listen beyond words to the essence of what is being spoken. It provides for greater mutual understanding and depth of expression. It asks us to resist focusing on our initial response and verify verbally to ensure we receive the speaker's deeper meaning.

Examples of reflective communication might be: I'm wondering if what you are saying is that you wish things had turned out differently? It feels like you are saying you felt misunderstood - is that right? I sense that the feeling underneath the words might be that you felt inspired to go another direction - is that true?

Desired Feelings
Understanding, Compassion, Empathy, Curiosity, Connection

How would I feel if someone offered me this kind of listening?

What quality do I need to cultivate to try listening this way?

Would reflective listening enable me to connect more deeply with others?

Can I extend this gift to myself and others by slowing down to listen on a deeper level?

Do I trust my intuition to look beyond someone's words?

Saying I Love You

The actual words "I love you" can be a powerful communication to yourself and others. Willingness to express these feelings out loud may be just the catalyst that is needed to initiate greater intimacy and connection in the moment. All of us have the need for expressions of love, and some more than others desire a spoken assurance.

Even communicating this with ourselves is a blessing, whether it is said to the child within, a part of us that is struggling or even our physical bodies, as they are all receptive to the words "I love you." There is great power in loving unconditionally, and verbalizing it brings it out in the open to be heard and felt.

Desired Feelings
Open-hearted, Connected, Expressive, Loving, Appreciated

Have I told myself how much I love and appreciate myself?

Are there those in my life that don't know how much I love them and would appreciate hearing it?

How often do I take the opportunity to write love notes to myself and others?

Can I see more opportunities to express the love in my heart?

Sharing Feedback with Love

There is love in being clear with others and at times we need to provide feedback regardless of how we think it will be received. Approaching feedback discussions with both kindness and direct, relevant information is possible. It may be that the other person is working in the dark as to what is expected, or unaware of how their choices are impacting another. Approaching a feedback conversation with the intent to establish safety for the discussion is a great first step. The love underlying the discussion is a critical guiding force and sharing that love as you open the conversation is of great value.

Communicating with specificity as to why something might not be working is also important. Afterwards, allowing the other person to fully express themselves without trying to shut down their feelings is honoring to them and can enable a new way of relating in difficult circumstances. Many times people simply need to be heard so that they can express their feelings without judgment to move through the experience and reach a new understanding.

Desired Feelings
Transparent, Clear, Direct, Peaceful, Expansive

Am I being honest with myself about how I feel?

Am I avoiding an uncomfortable conversation?

Am I able to approach this conversation with vulnerability and share my side of things?

Am I willing to listen without judgment and be curious?

Could I benefit from addressing the unstated discord rather than letting it drain my energy?

How would I want to be approached in this conversation?

Can I hold myself in love no matter how the other person perceives things?

Can I receive feedback without questioning my worth?

Sharing Feelings

Our feelings are an expression of our innermost world. Choosing to communicate them is a doorway to intimacy. Creating an inviting atmosphere through presence, openness and neutrality, we offer space for them to come forward. While feelings shift and change, sharing them in the moment is a deeply caring act. It gives room for them to be expressed and felt freely in our relationships.

Sometimes allowing our own feelings is a most difficult choice, especially when they are ones that we judge as negative such as grief, fear and anger. Sitting with them honestly can allow them to flow through us, opening a gateway to experiencing a shift. We can also see if there is a message behind them, approaching them with curiosity. When we ignore them we leave them to be stored in our bodies where they can impact our ability to relax, breathe and experience health. Allowing them to be felt in the body rather than suppressing them ensures they transform.

Desired Feelings
Authentic, Allowing, Welcome, Free, Understood

What are the ways I hold back emotions that are seeking expression?

Am I withholding feelings in my relationships?

How can I feel safe to express the ones that I am afraid of or resist? Would writing them out first on paper help?

Is there a friend who is willing to listen to me without trying to fix or fuel them?

Does recognizing that they are transitory help me face them?

Can I bring peace to myself or others through sharing or listening to feelings?

Can I invite others to share them more with me and be curious instead of reactive?

Sharing Ideas & Dreams

We can cultivate imagination, creativity and passion in our life by listening to our daydreams, ideas and inspirations. We are natural dreamers and sharing ideas and dreams allow us to connect from the mind and heart. If we have forgotten what it is like to dream, we can consciously set aside time to unhook from the world to let our minds wander freely. Cultivating our creative ideas or listening to our dreams can be self-loving and result in accessing previously untapped potential and information. As we extend a welcoming attitude to our ideas and others', we encourage dreams, creativity and inspiration to flow.

Verbally sharing our inner thoughts, dreams and desires are a courageous way to show up authentically and with vulnerability. It allows us to connect more deeply with others. Listening openly to another's ideas or dreams extends respect and invites intimacy. As we do this, we open up new dimensions of relating with others.

Desired Feelings
Engaged, Stimulated, Intrigued, Inspired, Curious, Hopeful

Have I given myself permission to let go of my ideas of being productive and lay in the grass and look at the sky?

Could I cultivate a willingness to be open to new dreams even if I don't know how they could come about?

How could I cultivate a home with open communication, non-judgment and support for the dreams of my family?

What would be a fun question to ask my loved one, so that I could learn more about their ideas or desires?

Sharing Laughter

Laughter has been called one of the most powerful medicines in life. Inviting in lightness, silliness, fun and joy through laughter is a powerful choice. Learning to laugh at ourselves, drop the heaviness and see the humor in life can be an amazing gift to ourselves and those around us. Laughing can lighten the mood, instigate fun and even improve our health.

Sharing a good laugh can come from telling a story, allowing ourselves to see the humor in life, watching a hilarious video or simply being infected by another's joy. Choosing to be the first to laugh at ourselves and be the model of not taking ourselves too seriously is a great gift. Telling jokes and drawing others out through the playful banter of this medium is a fun choice for all.

Desired Feelings
Laughter, Silly, Release, Joy, Relief

What can I do to invite more giggling and laughter into my life or the lives of those I love?

Can I see the humor in this situation to let my resistance go?

Have I had a good laugh lately?

What makes me feel silly and childlike, enough to let my hair down and have more fun?

Is having joy a priority in my life?

How do I make others laugh and can I cultivate it even more?

Sharing Stories

Stories are likely as old as language itself. For some of us, they are the means by which we love to share, even with ourselves! Being patient to receive and follow a story from beginning to end in its unfolding is a form of love through communication. Little children tell us stories as they form their first words to express their understanding of the world. Listening to a story unfold gives us a peek into the viewpoint, humor, awareness and interests of the teller.

Our own stories are also a treasure and we can benefit greatly from sitting down to write them out or share honestly with another our journey through life. It provides a sense of space for us to be ourselves without being rushed and to experience the joy of using our creativity in the telling.

Desired Feelings
Laughter, Enjoyment, Connection, Understanding, Creativity

What is in my heart that is unheard and seeking to be spoken?

How can I open myself to understanding more fully the experience of others around me?

How would it feel to daily give myself full attention for journaling and listening to my heart?

What would it mean to those I love to have my full, undivided attention when we share our day?

Would my family enjoy sharing stories at dinnertime?

Verbally Inviting Sexual Intimacy

Connecting through sex can be a profound act of intimacy or passion, playful exchange or a demonstration of love. Learning to cultivate loving ways to invite our partners to participate with us sexually may be more art than science. At the root of this invitation is the importance of seeking consent and cultivating sexual energy together. A primary assumption that is critical to hold is that no one ever owes us intimacy, and even in a long-term partnership saying no is always an option. Getting comfortable communicating your desires or discussing your partners' desires is a loving choice. This foundation of respect allows us to meet on equal footing and open to authentic intimacy.

Verbalizing the invitation can be very loving for both partners as it eliminates the possibility of missed signals and subtle hints. When both come together seeking to find a win-win solution, it may open the door to a more harmonious experience. Learning to gracefully share and receive feedback in this setting is a tremendous skill.

Using invitational phrases such as the examples below can provide a gentle introduction to a sexual intimacy and address common challenges:

"Would you be open to…"

"I'd really love to…"

"How would you feel about setting a time for us to connect alone since we are both so busy?"

"I would love to, but it would be better for me when…"

"I'm feeling stressed. Could we start with a simple back massage?"

"Love to, and could you help me with this first so I can relax?"

"I wish I felt up to it right now -- but I just don't, to be honest. How about a rain check?"

"Thank you for being up front with me that you aren't ready. Is there something else you do feel up to?"

Perhaps creating a playful code word or sending a sexy note to say you are thinking of the other ahead of time could be a fun way to signal your interest. Establishing a way to communicate interest may allow more grace and receptivity in the relationship long term, even if there are aspects of daily life to address.

Note: When sexual intimacy seems more difficult than just adapting to schedules and daily life, seeking professional help to explore creative solutions to meeting both partners' desires, or addressing past trauma or physical limitations can open the door to an expansion of love and connection.

Desired Feelings
Appreciated, Expressive, Sensuous, Sexy, Loving

What could I do to cultivate my sexual energy and share it verbally with my partner?

Can I explore speaking to my partner about how I'm feeling about my sexual experience?

How can I playfully let my partner know I am inviting them to sexually connect?

How could I hold a "no" answer from my partner without taking it personally?

Would it be valuable to initiate a discussion about asking for and giving feedback related to sexuality?

Could I share with my partner what things help me feel most open to saying "Yes?"

Are there any challenges we are facing that could benefit from outside help in this area?

Words of Appreciation

Hearing specific words of appreciation for who we are, what we do or how we show up in the world, nurtures the soul. It encourages us to share more of ourselves in that very way we are recognized. Words of appreciation given to others can assist them to recognize their own gifts. Learning to praise authentically can be a superpower.

As we experience our own support and love through praise, we learn that we can go within to find balance, strength and joy. We find that we can stand on our own two feet even when others fail to see us clearly. In addition, this allows us to freely praise others without jealousy or comparison. Expressed sincerely, appreciation builds confidence and allows us to savor life, others and ourselves.

Desired Feelings
Seen, Relaxed, Appreciated, Encouraged, Embraced

What would it look like if I turned my inner voice into a cheerleader instead of a critic?

Have I thanked my body today for all it does for me?

How graceful could my day be if I started it off appreciating myself for who I am?

How could those around me be encouraged by my words of appreciation?

What could I praise today, in order to focus on what is working with our family, instead of what is wrong?

Words of Encouragement

Offering encouragement is a wonderful choice to enable and accelerate growth. It allows for us to pause and be bolstered along the journey rather than have to wait to be acknowledged at the end or never feel supported along the way. It allows us to capture the joy of accomplishment many times over and treasure our steps as sacred.

We can greatly bless ourselves and others with words that inspire or offer support. It assists us to move into feeling the joy of our journey, and not just doing things and moving onto the next moment. Especially when we are tackling difficult things in life, we all need more than a single vote of confidence. We have great power within us to be a force of love - not just to others, but to ourselves, through our choice of encouraging words.

Desired Feelings
Supported, Encouraged, Celebrated, Witnessed

What are three things I did well today that I can acknowledge before I go to sleep tonight?

What can I honor about my experience today, that would help me feel my own loving kindness?

What appreciations can I see and verbalize so as to encourage others?

When I see or experience struggle, what encouragement can I offer?

When discouraged, can I suspend judgment on how I'm doing and open myself to a new viewpoint?

Words of Praise

Every word of praise that is genuinely offered is a gift and can be deeply satisfying to hear. When we take the time to verbalize our progress or contribution, we honor how we individually show up in the world. So often, we desire simply to be seen and this is a loving way to say, "I see you and what you are bringing to the world." This can be a self-loving act or a verbal gift to others.

We strive so much for outcomes, oftentimes without stopping along the way to recognize what we are doing. Every time we speak up to offer words of praise, we create a moment of cherishing not just the result, but the effort, desire and intention behind what we see coming to fruition. Praise that is specific and comes with authenticity allows others to feel the truth of it and know it is not just flattery.

For many people, hearing praise in a public setting is a great sign of love to them. It can be especially significant for their loved one to say publicly, in their presence, that they are important and loved for who they are, what they do or how they show up day to day.

Desired Feelings
Acknowledged, Appreciated, Seen, Encouraged, Honored

If I chose to praise myself today, what would I pick to honor in myself?

How does my choice to praise others publicly affect them?

What are the specific things that I can praise others for that would feel so good for them to hear?

How often do I accept praise with a simple thank you and no other words?

Am I able to value my contribution without expecting perfection?

Written Words of Love

While there are more means than ever to write words of love, the satisfaction of seeing them with our own eyes remains unchanged. For some, the tangible evidence of written words may be highly valued beyond even hearing it verbally. There exists within us a desire at times to ground ourselves in things we can see, and written cards, notes, emails, texts and other methods of communication can often be saved, read again and treasured.

The act of expressing our feelings of love in written words is a valuable action. It helps us to clarify our feelings, focus our communication and openly appreciate what we enjoy with another. We can do this within our own internal world as well. Writing a love letter with specific reasons we appreciate and love ourselves can be a powerful practice to initiate a more self-loving relationship.

Desired Feelings
Open, Expressive, Treasured, Loving, Embraced, Seen

What do I really appreciate about myself today that I can journal?

If I wrote myself a small love letter regularly, how would it affect my sense of self?

Do I take time to pause and share my love in writing?

When I feel inspired or grateful, can I share it with the ones I love through a message?

How would it feel to take the leap and express my feelings of love authentically with others?

Would it be fun to mail a love letter as a surprise gift for a birthday or special occasion?

CHAPTER 5

Ways of Thinking

Caring For Our Anger

Anger is the innate response we experience when our boundaries or sense of fairness and justice are violated. It rises in us seeking care for an underlying wound we feel within. Whatever thoughts we have about it being 'good' or 'bad', it is healthier to pass through us rather than be suppressed. However, how we choose to work with the feeling can have a significant impact on how lovingly we relate to ourselves and others. Feelings are transitory, but seek to be heard and acknowledged first and foremost. They grow in intensity when left unattended. We can see them as our inner children, crying for attention and care. Anger can be worked through in a range of ways but the intent to care for the wound or pain underneath the anger is critical. Anger might need to be spoken out loud, visualized in some form until our feelings shift, written out for ourselves to hear, and many other possible expressions. But then we can care for ourselves by asking, what is hurting beneath the flames of anger? Our own compassion for the hurt underneath is the balm we seek. Once we have done this, it makes it immeasurably easier to speak with others about our feelings from a place of inner truth and balance.

Desired Feelings
Acknowledged, Understood, Loving, Valued, Peaceful

What if I allow myself to feel the anger fully until it passes?

How will caring for my anger first, allow me to approach my loved ones differently?

What can I try to move through my anger and express my hurt, rather than trapping it and slipping into depression?

Can I take a walk to care for my anger before I approach my partner to work this out?

If I explode in anger, can I forgive myself, apologize and move to naming the hurt I'm experiencing?

Will vulnerability guide me to a more powerful resolution than blame?

Can I express my anger without shaming others?

Curiosity

Love expressed is, in every form, is a type of attention or presence to the self. When we attune with curiosity to ourselves we signal that each aspect or part of ourselves is worthy of attention. The same happens with our loved ones. Our presence itself is an expression of love. If a part of us is calling for attention, it may show up as needy or be exaggerated in its expression if ignored. As we approach anything within us that we might have previously avoided looking at, our curiosity and attention open the door to a new dynamic of change. As we listen to ourselves, even the parts we don't like, we expand our capacity to do the same for others and they feel heard. Our ability to be present with others is a reflection of how we are with our own inner selves. The willingness to engage with genuine curiosity demonstrates to others their importance to us over our views, judgments and self-interest. We metaphorically wrap our arms around them with our interest and attention.

Desired Feelings
Engaged, Open, Receptive, Intrigued, Interested

What can I see within myself that is calling for attention?

Would self-inquiry and a neutral approach with my inner world assist me in coming to more peace?

Are there times in the day that I need to check in more often before responding to others?

Am I able to explore my inner landscape when things don't go as I planned?

What can I do to provide a more curious, listening approach to my partner or children?

What is a new area of their life that I can engage with them to show their importance to me?

Embracing Differences

While we enjoy sharing similarities with others, differences are the spice of life and highlight our unique characteristics. Choosing to embrace what is different with curiosity and openness can enhance our ties. Whether embracing what is our own quality that stands out in the crowd or another's, we offer validation for the wide variety of expressions to be welcomed, accepted and appreciated. Doing this can lead us to find a middle ground, learn to draw on it as a strength or find our differences in a relationship complement each other and provide a result that is greater than the sum of two parts. It provides a path of harmony and unity to embrace differences.

Desired Feelings
Respect, Open, Harmonious, Inclusive, Free, Accepted

What can I do to see that benefit or value each trait I have that makes me feel different?

Can I give myself permission to accept myself for who I am?

Can I offer this to others? How do the differences in my relationships add to my life?

If I could extend loving kindness to myself or another who felt uneasy about a part of themselves, what would it be?

Freedom / Room to Explore

Sometimes the greatest gift to ourselves is space. Room to explore, freedom to express, allowance for new ways of being, thinking or living. The same goes for those we love, as the soul seeks expansion and seeks to know itself, it calls for freedom and openness to fulfill that desire. We can demonstrate great love to ourselves and others by trusting the innate desire for this freedom and self-expression. While we may not always understand what surfaces within us and others, we can learn to hear it out, acknowledge it and explore how to support the underlying desire in a way that works within our lives. There is an innate respect that is communicated when we open to this process. It allows for the soul to be fully present in all its parts, rather than just the ones we are comfortable with historically.

Desired Feelings
Trust, Allowing, Surrender, Open, Exploratory

What areas have I been fearful of that make me want to control things in my life?

Where do I have the opportunity to surrender and allow the unfolding of life?

Where can I set clear intentions and then let go of the 'how' in my life?

Where could I allow my family more freedom or offer more trust that they are on their path?

How could I hold what is happening around me differently, so that I could be more relaxed as we experience change?

Can I surrender and move past fear into trust in the divine or life?

Forgiveness

Forgiveness is essentially a tool of acceptance and surrender. When we look inside and are able to let go of self-judgments, we bring love to a part of us that we rejected. The same is true for our relationship to judgments with others. If we can release our judgments, we free ourselves from staying in the energy of anger, victimhood and pain and accept what is. We do not need to feel that what happened is ok, but simply be open to surrendering to what is - and choosing compassion for ourselves and others regardless of the circumstances. We may need to spend time caring for our anger, pain or sense of loss in order to move to the step of forgiveness. It is a path to acknowledging that we do not always have the full picture or have to understand, but we do have a choice to hold on or let go of judgment. Our ability to grasp that each of us does the best we can in our circumstances, frees us from the suffering of believing in what we think ought to have happened.

Desired Feelings
Soft, Release, Peaceful, Surrender

What areas of my life do I still judge myself for and can I see that I did the best I could at the time?

Can I offer myself healing by letting go of a mentality of right and wrong?

Can I receive my own forgiveness by softening my heart?

Can I surrender to unconditional love in this situation?

What examples of forgiveness can I turn to for inspiration?

Have I been the recipient of forgiveness and can I offer the same?

Gratitude

Self-appreciation is the atmosphere of love that allows me to open and relax. Gratitude for who I am, and what I uniquely bring to the world fills my heart with love. Expressions of appreciation also engender more intimacy and connection with others. Being in touch with my own inherent soul's expression allows me to attract and express love openly in my life. When we are not feeling good, shifting our focus to any small thing we can appreciate no matter the size, can be the initial catalyst to shift us into a better feeling state. In relationships, focusing on what is genuinely appreciated on a daily basis is a powerful elixir for love to grow. It builds our esteem and confidence within and helps others do the same.

Desired Feelings
Grateful, Appreciation, Attentive, Positive, Blessed

What can I see in myself right now that has gone unnoticed?

If I could share one word of appreciation for myself and what I have experienced today, what would it be?

How does cultivating a focus of gratitude change my daily experience?

When I am suffering what small thing can I be grateful for to help me shift my feelings?

Non-Judgment

The essence of non-judgment is suspending our belief that we know everything about a given situation and what is best. It allows us to be the observer in our lives and see what is present, without being embroiled or wrapped up in the drama up close. It asks us to raise our perspective to a higher level and acknowledge what is, for now, present within us and our lives. It is an attitude of not having to fix anything in the moment. It often feels like space or allowing what is occurring in the now to be. We can imagine that there is an underlying intention that is understandable for any given thing, even when it shows up in a way we are tempted to name it as wrong. If we can suspend judgment up front, our openness can allow us to potentially see the underlying need in any situation that is seeking to come forward.

Desired Feelings
Allowing, Unity, Acceptance, Grace

Am I resisting something that is pushing to the surface within me?

How would I feel if I accepted myself fully just for today?

Can I withhold judgment on whether this situation is 'good' or 'bad' in my life?

Can I accept with compassion the resistance I feel?

Will accepting this moment free my energy and mind?

Does it help to recognize that non-judgment is not agreement?

Can I see my loved ones as fully worthy without needing them to change?

Remembrance

For some of us, special dates being honored are an important part of our lives. Whether it is a anniversary, birth, death, special meeting or achievement to remember, they hold significance for us. As we pause in life to honor, celebrate, remember or acknowledge an important moment in our own lives or those around us, we share a form of love. In the pause is an opportunity to review our lives, cherish the changes we experience, show respect or honor for another and appreciate the moments of life that have meaning for us. We offer recognition to those we love of their presence in our lives.

Desired Feelings
Honored, Cherished, Reflective, Present

What are the events or moments in life that I could enjoy cherishing more fully?

Have I honored my own feelings as I move through unique events in my life - both joyful and sad ones?

What could help me create a more memorable experience with those I love?

What is important to my partner or child that I can bring my presence to?

Am I willing to slow down my life to cherish it?

Will it bring me more enjoyment and moments to remember?

Respect for Who I Am

The world is filled with diversity and variation, which includes me. The unique experience, preferences and views of each person make the world richer for the differences. Respecting these rather than trying to create sameness lends to each feeling treasured in relationship. Whether it is learning to respect what rises within us that is different, or acknowledging the range of experience in others that is unlike our own, we find harmony through acceptance. Sometimes we do not understand the perspective or tastes of another, but seeking to understand from curiosity rather than judgment, supports everyone involved. When we judge others, it is often a reflection that there is something in us we do not want to look at and have rejected. As we take the step to accept and love our own preferences, we have respect and love for others when they differ from us. We may consider that respect is giving others the same right as we ourselves have to express regardless of our agreement with another.

Desired Feelings
Acceptance, Allowing, Embraced, Open, Valued

When I sense I am different from those around me, can I assure myself that it is ok and I am loved?

Am I allowing myself to express my preferences and follow them in life?

When I am in relationship, do I trust that harmony can be established among diverse opinions or ways of living?

How can I seek to accept or understand rather than judge another?

Respecting Choices & Desires

Sometimes looking at our desires or accepting choices without judgment is a window for love. Choices may not look the same in retrospect, but we can offer acknowledgment that we or others did the best we could at the time. Choosing to respect a choice, signals the willingness to let each of us learn from our experience, understanding that we walk unique paths and have individual lessons to learn. No matter where we go in a single step, we are ultimately heading towards growth and the expansion of our soul. Similarly, desires are a guidepost from the soul to direct us, and although we don't always understand them, it is deeply loving to embrace and respect them. Offering ourselves the space to feel our desires without judgment, gives us a window to open to exploring how to fulfill them. Sometimes they scare us but we can open to seeing a way to integrate them in our lives, without ignoring or suppressing them. In intimate relationships, the same can be said for acknowledging the desires of others. Working together to negotiate solutions to meet the desires of both parties, creates a powerful opportunity for fulfillment and a more expansive relationship.

Desired Feelings
Respect, Peace, Flexible, Free, Acceptance

What feelings or desires have I been afraid to look at?

How could I nurture them by taking a first small step?

What choices have I judged in my life or others that I can let go of?

Can I see that I really didn't know better at the time?

What if I recognized that I have limited information about the path of others - would it allow me to be more at peace with their decisions?

Can I accept the diversity of desires in myself and those around me as beautiful and not fearful?

Showing Faith & Belief in Me

I am worthy of faith and there is universal support for my life path. I can choose to believe in myself and others, as we are all ultimately heading towards enlightenment no matter how long it takes. By choosing to see the light within myself and others, I anchor in the knowing that there is an indistinguishable divinity to all. As I express belief and encouragement, I provide fuel for this light to ignite and burn more brightly. Sometimes we need only be reminded it is there, to accelerate our growth and understanding. Our confidence in an inner light (even when unspoken is felt by those around us, and it provides a springboard to enable the next step. It is ok if we forget for a time how powerful we are, but the truth of it is - we cannot change the fact that we are divine beings in this human experience. The underlying essence of who we are is powerful and worthy of confidence.

Desired Feelings
Confident, Optimistic, Encouragement, Support

What do I see to believe in that feels expansive, open and enables me to be at peace in my life?

How can I hold my divine nature or capacity in my mind, as I face the unknown path before me?

How does it feel to imagine being on the other side of this challenge, having navigated it with ease?

What would enable me to expand my thinking and see the possibilities that my loved one can succeed at what is before them?

How can I express my support and encouragement in their core capacity to tackle whatever comes their way?

What would I want to hear, see or feel - if I was facing the same challenge?

Working with Fear

Fear is an undeniable feeling we all experience, and how we learn to relate to it impacts our stress level and happiness greatly. We can learn to hear the fundamental concern inside without letting it turn into a story that amplifies into more fear. There are a variety of ways to work with fear, but seeing it as only one possibility and not the whole truth is a great start. Our bodies benefit greatly from working it out of us, which might happen through physical activity, writing it out and shredding the writing, playing devil's advocate with the fearful ideas to help us determine what is actually true or what thoughts bring us relief and peace. At times, we may simply have to hold on in a dark moment to a single hopeful thought, reminding ourselves that it will pass. We can learn to acknowledge fear and it's existence, without giving it permission to drive our decisions or be the only voice in our head. We might benefit from exploring it as something outside of us, that we can see as separate from us as we sort out what we choose to believe.

Desired Feelings
Hope, Faith, Trust, Peace, Calm

Is it possible that this thought is not entirely true?

If I could choose a response to my fear, what brings me the most relief and peace in this moment?

How is fear serving me and where is it becoming debilitating?

How can I encourage my mind to hold to other possibilities as I face the unknown?

What activities take me out of the paralysis of fear - cleaning, exercise, breathing, writing, music?

What choices do I have to face my fear?

If there is no action to take, can I surrender to the divine in trust?

Will journaling help me observe what leads to peace vs. anxiety in myself so I can learn from it?

CHAPTER 6

Ways of Touching

Caressing

Caressing can be both a beautiful, gentle, comforting action or a sensuous, stimulating touch. The giver's focus or purpose behind the touch is what guides to these results. A caress is typically given as a light touch approaching another with care. In response, receiving a caress with love may be done by relaxing, thanking the giver or even encouraging them with a sigh or sound of appreciation.

Melting into the caress of another, allowing the body to relax and open to the moment can be blissful. Both giver and receiver can benefit from the exchange of energy, love and touch. Exploring different types of caressing touch can be a fun tactile exploration for both parties and help build deeper bonds.

Note: Asking for permission to touch rather than implying consent is always suggested.

Desired Feelings
Pleasure, Sensual, Loving, Appreciated, Caring, Connected

What is the touch I love and so enjoy receiving?

How could I communicate that quality?

When I receive a caress, am I allowing myself to pause and enjoy it?

How would it feel to explore different ways of caressing with another?

When I am touching another, what am I intending them to receive?

Have I had fun lately playing in the sensuous world of touch?

Cuddling

Human touch is a way we relate to life from the moment we are born. It offers us a vehicle to explore, as well as give and receive affection. Simply by snuggling on the couch or cuddling in bed, we connect biologically and emotionally. For some of us, touch is a primary mode of connection that fosters a feeling of security and love.

When we support our need for touch we fulfill a basic need and ground ourselves in our bodies. Sometimes words feel inadequate and touch can communicate beyond what we can say and offer reassurance, comfort and love. A full body cuddle can be the most delicious support to our emotions, heart and nervous system.

Note: Asking for permission to touch rather than implying consent is always suggested. For example: Are you interested in snuggling?

Desired Feelings
Connected, Nurtured, Grounded, Relaxed, Comforted, Appreciated

Where can I enjoy more affectionate touch in my life?

Can I express to others my desire for it or initiate it?

Do I greet others I love openly with affection?

How can I incorporate more opportunities to enjoy physical connection with my family to express my love?

How does having adequate non-sexual touch affect my sexual life? Does it help me make better choices?

Holding Hands

Holding hands creates a physical link between us that can be symbolic of everything from a show of safety or protection to an enduring romantic connection that is deep and strong. It can be a sign of compassion, tenderness, companionship, friendship or be a signal of arousal or desire for further intimacy. When done in love, we feel the extending of the self towards another in the act. As holding hands literally connects our bodies, we find our souls expressing the desire to merge for that moment with another.

Note: Asking for permission to touch rather than implying consent is always suggested. For example: Can I take your hand?

Desired Feelings
Protected, Important, Connected, Loved, Supported

Am I open to the public display of love my partner is offering?

Would offering my hand open the door to connection?

Could the squeeze of my hand signal support and love?

What support and love have I received through the simple gesture of hand-holding?

Can I freely connect in touch and let go, trusting all is well?

Holding Me When I'm Hurting

Sometimes when we are mentally suffering or in pain emotionally, we seek physical comfort. Each of us may desire to be held in comfort at these times. Asking to be held or offering to hold another without trying to fix their pain is an act of pure love. While we may prefer another to do this for us, in those times we are alone, even choosing to wrap ourselves in a soft blanket with a soft candle or music surrounding us may ease our pain and send a signal within that we are loved. There are times when physical comfort is the most direct and helpful act of love. We may need to ask if this is the case, or tell others that is what we desire, but it is a simple choice and a means to love and providing comfort.

Note: Asking for permission to touch rather than implying consent is always suggested. For example: I'd like to hold you, are you open to that?

Desired Feelings
Supported, Safe, Comforted, Nurtured, Connected

Do I feel able to ask for what I need in difficult times?

Can I take a small step to change any patterns of isolation I might have when suffering?

Would the comfort of a hug or holding another's hand in my pain or grief help me feel less alone?

If I'm not sure it is wanted, am I willing to be vulnerable and ask for or offer a hug?

Hugging

The action of a physical embrace is a beautiful gesture of love. A hug is akin to the coming of two hearts together as we physically connect facing one another. Like many acts of affection, a hug can mean many things, but its essence is to wrap another person in our loving. It could be the love of friendship, love of a parent or child, romantic love, and even the love of one stranger to another for simply being human. It is a universal sign of connection and we can explore how to share and receive it best. Some people seek a gentle touch, others a tight embrace, and some a long sensuous hug. All of these are enhanced by our ability to show up for that embrace with full attention and presence, communicating our affection with our eyes and heart.

Note: Asking for permission to touch rather than implying consent is always suggested. For example, Can I give you a hug?

Desired Feelings
Warmth, Embraced, Loving, Caring, Contained, Safe, Welcomed

What is the type of hug I love to share?

How can I offer my love in a hug with more attentiveness or presence?

When I am being hugged, do I receive it fully or quickly pull away?

Would it be fun to explore different ways of hugging with my loved ones?

What helps me to show up with warmth and welcoming in my hug?

Have I embraced another openly with the true exuberance I feel inside?

How much joy do I share when I am open with my love?

Kissing

A kiss offers the recipient a very intimate meeting of the soul when lip to lip. A tender kiss on the head or hand might be cherishing another rather than romantic in nature, but still a deeply heart-filled action. While it is possible to be surprised by a kiss, generally we meet in mutual loving expression with the act. Kissing, when explored as a sensory tool, can offer a wide range of experiences from the wildly erotic to a simple playful, platonic connection. Taking time in a romantic relationship to connect with kissing and not rush past the act, can be a deeply satisfying action to enjoy together. As a public expression, it may signal to another that we are happy to acknowledge our love for them anywhere, anytime.

Note: Asking for permission to touch rather than implying consent is always suggested.

Desired Feelings
Aroused, Sweet, Tender, Passionate, Playful, Appreciated

When is the last time I paused to enjoy kissing for the sake of it?

Have I given my family a heartfelt kiss of affection today?

What ways of kissing can I offer my partner to playfully meet them?

Can I ask for and allow myself to be covered in kisses head to toe?

How could I give or receive each kiss with greater attentiveness and appreciation?

Massage

Physical touch is a primary way to communicate love and attention. It aids us to be present in our bodies, let go of mental activity, relax and feel pleasure. Focusing on giving and receiving pleasure through massage can be a blessing to both parties. We all exist within bodies filled with vast networks of nerves that can be nourished and calmed by touch. This is particularly acknowledged as important for the development of infants and children. We may find it to be just as valued by adults for different reasons.

Whether part of a platonic or romantic relationship, it nourishes our need for pleasure and physical connection. This leads to relaxation which supports a healthy immune system and overall well-being. Communication about specific preferences for type of touch or discussing the intentions of the giver and receiver can be a significant help to creating a beautiful moment of sensory pleasure and physical nourishment.

Note: Asking for permission to touch rather than implying consent is always suggested.

Desired Feelings
Nourished, Healthy, Relaxed, Restored, Refreshed

How can I bring more touch through massage into my life?

Can I sense how it affects my sense of well-being and health to receive it?

Would I like to share my preferences with my partner up front or give them positive feedback along the way?

How does getting enough physical contact affect me and the choices I make?

Can I sense my loved one's pleasure and relaxation as I give them a massage?

Is there a small activity like rubbing the feet that we could introduce at the end of our day to help us unwind?

Non-Sexual Physical Touch

Connecting through the physical body offers a visible, tactile sign of love. This is a means of expression that is desired as it is tangible and pleasurable. All human beings have a need for consistent loving touch. Touch allows us to express beyond words and share warmth and actually exchange our energy. Cultivating a relationship of touch for ourselves and with others supports our physical well-being and happiness. Asking permission to touch may be appropriate, and whether or not it is received in that moment, it is a loving expression on its own.

Note: Asking for permission to touch rather than implying consent is always suggested.

Desired Feelings
Nourished, Nurtured, Supported, Loving, Welcomed, Relaxed

What types of physical contact do those I love welcome and enjoy most?

Can I ask for the touch I need in order to feel connected and loved?

Am I willing to say, "no thank you" to physical contact when it does not feel good?

Can I ask others for permission when I am unsure if contact is desired?

Do I have healthy boundaries that make me feel good in this area?

What places in my life offer more opportunities for nurturing touch?

Public Expressions of Affection

The authentic expression of affection in public signals to the world the shared intimacy that is occurring within a relationship. It can be significant to one party or both that this is openly expressed. It might be a signal to them that you are proud to be with them or fulfill the desire for equal authenticity in all settings. Whatever the case, it might be a valuable point of conscious discussion to support each person in the relationship. The outward flow of joy that is expressed in public affection can be a seed of joy for others - for them to realize they also desire that exchange or remind them of the sweetness that love can offer in a moment of life.

Note: Asking for permission to touch rather than implying consent is always suggested.

Desired Feelings
Honored, Respected, Proud, Open, Authentic, Free

How do I feel about physical affection in public?

Am I being myself in those interactions?

Am I in touch with myself / body when interacting with others?

Do I allow myself to show my true affections in a public setting?

Do I show up in my own authentic way of loving or hold back for fear of what others may think?

Do I have stories in my mind about what is appropriate and does that feel true to me?

Reconnecting with Touch

Many of us are physically oriented in how we relate to the world, and find touch to be a highly valued way of loving. Making it a priority to stop what we are doing to share a heartfelt hug, offer a tender kiss or exchange another tangible gift of affection can be very reassuring and connecting. When we have been away from each other or are simply coming home from the day to reenter our shared living space with another, it can be a ritual of warmth to extend oneself in this way.

The intent with which we touch has an important impact on the exchange of it. Being fully present, looking the other in the eye, intending to connect with love are all beneficial to the process of reintegrating into relationship after being apart. A truly exuberant embrace when reconnecting, may be the expression of joy that speaks volumes of our love for another.

Note: Asking for permission to touch rather than implying consent is always suggested.

Desired Feelings
Celebratory, Connected, Warmth, Welcomed, Nurtured

What are the ways I can offer my love through physical connection?

Would my relationship benefit from more loving touch?

Do I need to make time to be physically connected a priority?

Did I ask for permission and give room for my loved one to say yes or no to touch in their own timing?

What ritual could we instill after being apart that would help us come together again?

Sexual / Sensual Touch

Physical intimacy is an important expression of love. It is a reflection of sharing our innermost self and romantic feelings. Whether it is sensual or sexual, pleasure can be found in a wide spectrum of ways when we put our focus on cultivating it. We may find that we need to be rested and relaxed to fully embrace it. Being aware of your own body and breath before connecting with a partner tends to offer time to give and receive more fully in the moment of touch.

We may need only sensual touch at times, and may benefit from communicating this to our partner to support one another. Not setting expectations on an end goal of sexual climax is often helpful to allowing sensation to guide the experience and lead to genuine connection and pleasure without pressure. Simply focusing on body sensations and letting go of thinking can be a powerful element of a positive sensual or sexual experience. Learning to communicate about touch in an encouraging way is a great skill to help both partners get comfortable and share more pleasure. Intimate partners are likely to benefit from verbalizing their desires, and discussing how to meet and respect any differences.

Note: Asking for permission to touch rather than implying consent is always suggested.

If one partner has had prior experiences with sexual trauma or other painful experiences, couples may benefit from seeking help to move through the spontaneous body responses and emotions that can arise from touch in the present moment. A loving touch from a partner can sometimes be the first safe place that physical pain or denied emotions from prior experiences arise seeking to be healed. Pausing with compassion to allow for these expressions to move up and out provides a key step towards healing.

Desired Feelings
Pleasure, Ecstasy, Excited, Treasured, Stimulated, Loving, Relaxed

Do I set time aside to cultivate my own sexual energy and bring sensuality into my life?

What actions help me get into my body and out of my head to allow for more pleasure?

Do I ask for what I need and use words of encouragement to help my partner know what works for me?

Can I equally initiate sexual play and respect boundaries?

How can I cultivate more pleasure by using all my senses?

Am I comfortable speaking about sexuality with my partner and children as needed?

What elements of my sexual life are seeking more attention?

Do I need any support to grow in this area and have a more satisfied sexual life?

Am I working with any difficult feelings, judgments, pain or fears that lend themselves to seeking professional support?

CHAPTER 7

Discovering Your Ways of Loving

Discover Your *Ways of Loving*

To identify your *Ways of Loving,* you can use the following worksheets in this chapter or go to our free, short tutorial at:

http://www.thelovemandala.com/more/

In this chapter, I will walk you through an easy process to help you uncover the most important ways you desire to be loved at this time in your life. This can empower you to communicate your *Ways of Loving* and open to experiencing more love. By inviting your loved to follow the process, you open the door to understand them and create more powerfully loving experiences between you.

Step 1: Check up to sixteen of the top feelings you want to experience on page 90.

Step 2: Use the chart on page 91 to narrow down your top desired feelings to four desired feelings.

Step 3: Go through Pages 92-105 and mark your top four desired feelings on the left hand side of each page.

Please Note: Some desired feelings are associated with all *Ways* and others only one or two. Feel free to amend your list if you think of a *Way of Loving* that is not listed or in is another section but feels right to you. These are just my top suggestions.

Step 4: Evaluate on pages 92-105 which *Ways of Loving* in the right hand column are most meaningful to you that evoke the feelings you highlighted. You can flip through the book to read about each way to help you decide. Circle or highlight them once you pick.

Please Note: You may find that one or more of your *Ways of Loving* are about relating to yourself more than other people.

Step 5: List your current *Ways of Loving* on page 106. Then share your results to explore how you can create more love and connection with yourself, partner, family or friends. Page 107 provides room to list the *Ways of Loving* of your loved ones.

Step 1: Check up to **sixteen** of the top desired feelings you want to experience on this list.

Desired Feelings

☐ Abundant	☐ Excited	☐ Powerful
☐ Acceptance	☐ Expansive	☐ Present
☐ Acknowledged	☐ Exploratory	☐ Protected
☐ Allowing	☐ Expressive	☐ Proud
☐ Appreciation	☐ Faith	☐ Receptive
☐ Aroused	☐ Flexible	☐ Reflective
☐ Attentive	☐ Focused	☐ Relaxed
☐ Authentic	☐ Free	☐ Release
☐ Aware	☐ Fun	☐ Relief
☐ Balanced	☐ Generous	☐ Resourceful
☐ Blessed	☐ Gentle	☐ Restored
☐ Calm	☐ Gracious	☐ Respected
☐ Capable	☐ Grateful	☐ Responsible
☐ Caring	☐ Grounded	☐ Safe
☐ Celebratory	☐ Happy	☐ Satisfied
☐ Centered	☐ Harmonious	☐ Seen
☐ Charitable	☐ Healthy	☐ Sensual
☐ Cherished	☐ Heard	☐ Sexy
☐ Clear	☐ Heartfelt	☐ Soft
☐ Collaborative	☐ Honest	☐ Solace
☐ Comforted	☐ Honored	☐ Spacious
☐ Compassion	☐ Hopeful	☐ Spontaneity
☐ Competent	☐ Inclusive	☐ Steady
☐ Complete	☐ Innovative	☐ Stimulated
☐ Confident	☐ Inspired	☐ Strong
☐ Connected	☐ Integrated	☐ Supported
☐ Consoled	☐ Intrigued	☐ Surprised
☐ Contained	☐ Intimate	☐ Surrender
☐ Cooperative	☐ Joyful	☐ Sweet
☐ Creative	☐ Kind	☐ Tender
☐ Curious	☐ Laughter	☐ Transparent
☐ Direct	☐ Lightness	☐ Treasured
☐ Ecstasy	☐ Non-Attachment	☐ Trust
☐ Embraced	☐ Nurtured/Nourished	☐ Understanding
☐ Empathy	☐ Open	☐ Unity
☐ Empowered	☐ Open-Hearted	☐ Unquestioned
☐ Encouraged	☐ Optimistic	☐ Valued
☐ Energized	☐ Patience	☐ Warmth
☐ Engaged	☐ Passionate	☐ Welcomed
☐ Enjoyment	☐ Peaceful	☐ Whole
☐ Entertained	☐ Playful	☐ Witnessed
☐ Enthusiastic	☐ Pleasure	☐ Worthy
☐ Evolving	☐ Positive	

Step 2: Follow the steps below to identify the most desired feelings to you, **narrowing down to your top four**. Do this by starting with up to sixteen feelings on the left hand side of the chart. Reduce these to eight in the middle column and then your final four selections in the right hand side.

Step 3 & 4: Mark your top **four desired feelings** on the <u>left</u> <u>hand</u> <u>column</u> of pages 92–105. Evaluate which *Ways of Loving* in the <u>right hand column</u> are the most meaningful to evoke that feeling for you. You can flip through the book to read about each way to help you decide. Each *Way of Loving* is alphabetized within it's section of the book.

For your reference, the *Way of Loving* section that they come from is noted in bold: Way of Acting, Being, Speaking, Thinking or Touching.

Desired Feelings   Ways of Loving

Abundant

Acting: Financial Support **Being:** Allowing Space or Time Alone **Thinking:** Gratitude

Acceptance

Being: Accepting all of Me, Patience, Self-Awareness, Wholeness **Thinking:** Embracing Differences, Forgiveness, Respect For Who I Am

Acknowledged

Speaking: Acknowledging / Allowing Feelings **Thinking:** Apologizing, Reflective Listening, Words of Encouragement, Words of Praise **Touching:** Caring for Our Anger, Gratitude, Working with Fear

Allowing

Being: Accepting All of Me, Allowing Space or Time Alone, Cultivating Trust, Patience, Surrender **Thinking:** Freedom / Room to Explore

Appreciation

Being: Recognizing My Inherent Worth **Speaking:** Saying I Love You, Words of Appreciation, Words of Praise, Written Words of Love **Thinking:** Gratitude

Aroused

Speaking: Sharing Feelings, Verbally Inviting Sexual Intimacy **Touching:** Caressing, Kissing, Sexual / Sensual Touch

Attentive

Being: Attentiveness, Being Present, Listening From the Heart, Self-Awareness **Speaking:** Reflective Listening **Touching:** Caressing, Cuddling, Holding Hands, Holding Me When I'm Hurting, Hugging

Authentic

Being: Being Present, Listening from the Heart, I am Love, Vulnerability **Speaking:** Asking For What you Want, Authentic Honest Communication, Communicating During Conflict, Sharing Feelings

Desired Feelings   Ways of Loving

Aware
Being: Being Present, Listening from the Heart, Self-Awareness **Thinking:** Caring for Our Anger, Working with Fear

Balanced
Acting: Physical Care **Being:** Holding My Center In Love Thinking: Caring for Our Anger, Working with Fear

Blessed
Being: Elevating Your Feeling State **Speaking:** Words of Appreciation, Written Words of Love **Thinking:** Gratitude

Calm
Being: Allowing Space or Time Alone, Being Present **Thinking:** Working with Fear

Capable
Acting: Accountability / Self Responsibility **Being:** Boundaries, Elevating Your Feeling State **Thinking:** Showing Faith & Belief in Me

Caring
Acting: Attentiveness, Kindness **Being:** Holding My Center In Love, Listening From the Heart **Speaking:** Reflective Listening **Thinking:** Caring for Our Anger **Touching:** Caressing, Cuddling, Holding Hands, Holding Me When I'm Hurting, Hugging

Celebratory
Being: Recognizing My Inherent Worth, Wholeness **Speaking:** Sharing Stories, Words of Appreciation, Words of Encouragement, Written Words of Love **Thinking:** Respect For Who I Am **Touching:** Hugging, Kissing

Centered
Being: I am Love, Being Present, Allowing Space or Time Alone, Holding My Center in Love

Charitable
Acting: Acts of Service, Financial Support

Cherished
Acting: Cherishing Through Eye Gazing **Being:** Listening From the Heart **Speaking:** Sharing Stories, Words of Appreciation, Words of Encouragement **Thinking:** Embracing Differences, Remembrance, Respect For Who I Am **Touching:** Caressing, Cuddling, Hugging, Kissing, Sexual / Sensual Touch

Desired Feelings   Ways of Loving

Clear — **Being:** Boundaries, Holding My Center in Love, Self-Awareness **Speaking:** Asking for What You Want, Reflective Listening, Sharing Feedback with Love

Collaborative — **Acting:** Sharing in Activities **Speaking:** Reflective Listening

Comforted — **Acting:** Kindness **Being:** Listening From the Heart, Showing Compassion, Surrender **Thinking:** Caring for Our Anger **Touching:** Cuddling, Holding Hands, Holding Me When I'm Hurting, Hugging

Compassion — **Being:** Holding Space for Others, Patience, Showing Compassion **Thinking:** Caring for Our Anger

Competent — **Acting:** Accountability / Self Responsibility, Supporting Learning and Growth **Thinking:** Showing Faith & Belief in Me

Complete — **Being:** Recognizing My Inherent Worth, Wholeness **Speaking:** Reflective Listening **Thinking:** Embracing Differences

Confident — **Being:** Elevating Your Feeling State **Speaking:** Words of Encouragement **Thinking:** Showing Faith & Belief in Me

Connected — **Acting:** Cherishing Through Eye Gazing, Sharing in Activities **Being:** Accepting All of Me, Being Present, Listening From the Heart, Wholeness **Speaking:** Authentic / Honest Communication, Reflective Listening, Saying I Love You, Sharing Stories, Words of Appreciation **Touching:** Caressing, Cuddling, Holding Hands, Holding Me When I'm Hurting, Hugging, Kissing, Public Expressions of Affection, Reconnecting with Touch

Consoled — **Being:** Showing Compassion **Thinking:** Caring for Our Anger, Working with Fear **Touching:** Holding Me When I'm Hurting, Hugging

Contained — **Being:** Cultivating Trust **Thinking:** Caring for Our Anger **Touching:** Cuddling, Holding Me When I'm Hurting, Hugging

Desired Feelings   Ways of Loving

Cooperative

Being: Cultivating Trust **Speaking:** Communicating During Conflict **Thinking:** Embracing Differences

Creative

Acting: Creative Play, Surprises / Unexpected Gifts **Being:** Allowing Space or Time Alone, Elevating Your Feeling State **Speaking:** Sharing Ideas and Dreams, Sharing Stories

Curious

Being: Self-Awareness **Speaking:** Reflective Listening, Sharing Ideas and Dreams **Thinking:** Curiosity

Direct

Speaking: Authentic / Honest Communication, Communicating During Conflict, Sharing Feedback with Love

Ecstasy

Touching: Caressing, Kissing, Sexual / Sensual Touch

Embraced

Being: Acknowledging / Allowing Feelings, Accepting All of Me, Listening From the Heart, Recognizing My Inherent Worth, Self-Awareness, Wholeness **Speaking:** Words of Appreciation, Written Words of Love **Thinking:** Embracing Differences, Respect For Who I Am **Touching:** Cuddling, Holding Me When I'm Hurting, Hugging

Empathy

Being: Showing Compassion **Speaking:** Reflective Listening, Sharing Feelings **Touching:** Holding Me When I'm Hurting

Empowered

Acting: Accountability / Self Responsibility **Being:** Elevating Your Feeling State, Holding My Center in Love **Speaking:** Words of Appreciation, Words of Encouragement, Words of Praise

Encouraged

Acting: Supporting Learning & Growth **Being:** Allowing Space or Time Alone, Listening From the Heart **Speaking:** Sharing Ideas & Dreams, Words of Appreciation, Words of Encouragement, Words of Praise **Thinking:** Embracing Differences

Energized

Acting: Creative Play **Being:** Elevating Your Feeling State **Speaking:** Sharing Ideas & Dreams, Sharing Laughter, Words of Appreciation, Words of Encouragement

Desired Feelings　Ways of Loving

Engaged
Acting: Sharing in Activities **Being:** Being Present **Speaking:** Sharing Ideas and Dreams **Thinking:** Curiosity

Enjoyment
Acting: Sharing in Activities **Being:** Elevating Your Feeling State **Speaking:** Sharing Stories **Touching:** Caressing, Cuddling, Hugging, Kissing, Sexual / Sensual Touch

Entertained
Acting: Activating Joy & Fun **Speaking:** Sharing Laughter, Sharing Stories

Enthusiastic
Acting: Activating Joy & Fun **Being:** Elevating Your Feeling State **Speaking:** Sharing Laughter, Sharing Ideas & Dreams, Written Words of Love

Evolving
Acting: Supporting Learning & Growth **Being:** Elevating Your Feeling State **Speaking:** Words of Appreciation, Words of Encouragement **Thinking:** Respect for Who I Am, Freedom / Room to Explore

Excited
Acting: Activating Joy & Fun, Surprises / Unexpected Gifts **Speaking:** Sharing Ideas and Dreams, Verbally Inviting Sexual Intimacy **Touching:** Caressing, Cuddling, Kissing, Sexual / Sensual Touch

Expansive
Acting: Supporting Learning & Growth **Being:** Allowing Space or Time Alone, Elevating Your Feeling State, I am Love **Speaking:** Words of Appreciation, Words of Encouragement **Thinking:** Respect for Who I Am, Freedom / Room to Explore, Curiosity

Exploratory
Acting: Creative Play **Being:** Allowing Space or Time Alone, Elevating Your Feeling State, Self-Awareness **Speaking:** Sharing Ideas and Dreams, Verbally Inviting Sexual Intimacy **Thinking:** Freedom/Room to Explore, Curiosity **Touching:** Caressing, Non-sexual Touch, Sexual / Sensual Touch

Expressive
Acting: Creative Play **Speaking:** Authentic / Honest Communication, Saying I Love You, Sharing Ideas and Dreams, Sharing Laughter, Sharing Stories, Words of Appreciation, Written Words of Love **Touching:** Caressing, Cuddling, Hugging, Massage, Non-sexual Touch, Sexual / Sensual Touch

Desired Feelings   Ways of Loving

Harmonious
Being: I am Love, Holding My Center In Love, Cultivating Trust   **Thinking:** Caring for Our Anger, Embracing Differences, Non-Judgment, Respect For Who I Am

Healthy
Acting: Physical Care   **Being:** Elevating Your Feeling State   **Thinking:** Caring for Our Anger   **Touching:** Caressing, Cuddling, Hugging, Massage, Non-sexual Touch, Sexual / Sensual Touch

Heard
Being: Acknowledging / Allowing Feelings, Attentiveness   **Speaking:** Authentic / Honest Communication   **Thinking:** Respect For Who I Am

Heartfelt
Acting: Cherishing Through Eye Gazing   **Being:** Listening From the Heart   **Speaking:** Authentic / Honest Communication, Saying I Love You, Written Words of Love

Honest
Being: Self-Awareness, Vulnerability   **Speaking:** Authentic / Honest Communication, Asking for What You Want   **Thinking:** Caring for Our Anger

Honored
Being: Attentiveness, Being Present, Cultivating Trust   **Speaking:** Apologizing, Authentic Honest Communication, Words of Appreciation, Words of Praise   **Thinking:** Gratitude, Remembrance, Respect For Who I Am   **Touching:** Caressing, Cuddling, Hugging, Kissing, Massage, Non-sexual Touch, Sexual / Sensual Touch

Hopeful
Being: Elevating Your Feeling State   **Speaking:** Sharing Ideas and Dreams, Words of Encouragement   **Thinking:** Caring for Our Anger, Showing Faith & Belief in Me, Working with Fear

Inclusive
Acting: Building Traditions   **Being:** Accepting All of Me, Acknowledging / Allowing Feelings   **Thinking:** Embracing Differences, Respect For Who I Am

Innovative
Acting: Creative Play   **Being:** Elevating Your Feeling State   **Speaking:** Sharing Ideas and Dreams   **Thinking:** Curiosity

Desired Feelings   Ways of Loving

Faith

Being: Cultivating Trust **Speaking:** Words of Encouragement **Thinking:** Showing Faith & Belief in Me, Working with Fear

Flexible

Acting: Creative Play **Speaking:** Words of Encouragement **Thinking:** Freedom / Room to Explore, Respecting Choices & Desires

Focused

Acting: Attentiveness **Being:** Self-Awareness, Elevating Your Feeling State, Listening From the Heart

Free

Acting: Surprises / Unexpected Gifts **Being:** Allowing Space or Time Alone, Cultivating Trust **Thinking:** Freedom/Room to Explore, Respecting Choices & Desires

Fun

Acting: Activating Joy & Fun, Surprises / Unexpected Gifts **Speaking:** Sharing Stories **Touching:** Caressing, Cuddling, Hugging, Massage, Non-sexual Touch, Sexual / Sensual Touch

Generous

Acting: Acts of Service, Surprises / Unexpected Gifts **Being:** Listening From the Heart, Showing Compassion **Thinking:** Showing Faith & Belief in Me

Gentle

Acting: Gentleness, Kindness **Being:** Showing Compassion, Gentleness

Gracious

Acting: Acts of Service, Financial Support **Being:** Cultivating Trust, Patience **Thinking:** Non-Judgment

Grateful

Speaking: Words of Appreciation **Thinking:** Gratitude

Grounded

Acting: Building Traditions **Being:** Attentiveness, Being Present, Self-Awareness **Touching:** Caressing, Cuddling, Hugging, Kissing, Massage, Non-sexual Touch, Sexual / Sensual Touch

Happy

Acting: Activating Joy & Fun, Surprises / Unexpected Gifts **Being:** Elevating Your Feeling State **Speaking:** Sharing Laughter

Desired Feelings   Ways of Loving

Inspired

Acting: Creative Play **Being:** Elevating Your Feeling State Speaking: Sharing Ideas and Dreams **Thinking:** Curiosity, Respect For Who I Am, Showing Faith & Belief in Me

Integrated

Being: Being Present, Self-Awareness, Wholeness **Thinking:** Caring for Our Anger, Respect For Who I Am

Intrigued

Being: Attentiveness, Being Present **Speaking:** Sharing Ideas and Dreams **Thinking:** Curiosity

Intimate

Acting: Cherishing Through Eye Gazing **Being:** Attentiveness, Being Present **Speaking:** Saying I Love You, Verbally Inviting Sexual Intimacy, Written Words of Love **Touching:** Caressing, Cuddling, Hugging, Sexual / Sensual Touch

Joyful

Acting: Activating Joy & Fun, Surprises / Unexpected Gifts Being: Elevating Your Feeling State **Speaking:** Sharing Laughter, Written Words of Love **Touching:** Caressing, Cuddling, Hugging, Kissing, Massage, Non-sexual Touch, Sexual / Sensual Touch

Kind

Acting: Kindness **Being:** Showing Compassion, Gentleness

Laughter

Acting: Activating Joy & Fun, Surprises / Unexpected Gifts **Speaking:** Sharing Laughter, Sharing Stories

Lightness

Acting: Activating Joy & Fun, Surprises / Unexpected Gifts **Being:** Elevating Your Feeling State, Gentleness **Thinking:** Curiosity, Freedom / Room to Explore

Non-Attachment

Being: Showing Compassion, Surrender **Thinking:** Non-Judgment, Curiosity, Forgiveness, Respect For Who I Am, Respecting Choices & Desires

Nourished / Nurtured

Acting: Physical Care, Kindness **Being:** Accepting All of Me, Attentiveness, Cultivating Trust **Speaking:** Words of Encouragement, Written Words of Love **Thinking:** Caring for Our Anger, Showing Faith & Belief in Me **Touching:** Caressing, Cuddling, Holding Me When I'm Hurting, Hugging, Massage, Non-sexual Touch, Sexual / Sensual Touch, Reconnecting with Touch

Desired Feelings	Ways of Loving
Open	**Acting:** Cherishing Through Eye Gazing **Being:** Gentleness, Surrender, Vulnerability **Speaking:** Authentic / Honest Communication, Sharing Feelings **Thinking:** Curiosity, Embracing Differences, Freedom / Room to Explore, Respect For Who I Am, Respecting Choices & Desires
Open-Hearted	**Acting:** Building Traditions, Kindness **Being:** Listening From the Heart, Showing Compassion, Vulnerability **Speaking:** Saying I Love You, Sharing Feelings
Optimistic	**Being:** Elevating Your Feeling State **Speaking:** Words of Encouragement **Thinking:** Showing Faith & Belief in Me, Working with Fear
Patience	**Being:** Patience **Speaking:** Words of Encouragement **Thinking:** Showing Faith & Belief in Me
Passionate	**Speaking:** Saying I Love You, Sharing Feelings, Verbally Inviting Sexual Intimacy, Written Words of Love **Touching:** Hugging, Kissing, Sexual / Sensual Touch
Peaceful	**Being:** Being Present, Holding my Center In Love, Patience **Speaking:** Apologizing **Thinking:** Caring for Our Anger, Forgiveness, Working with Fear
Playful	**Acting:** Activating Joy & Fun, Surprises / Unexpected Gifts **Speaking:** Sharing Laughter, Sharing Stories **Thinking:** Curiosity, Freedom / Room to Explore **Touching:** Caressing, Cuddling, Kissing
Pleasure	**Acting:** Activating Joy & Fun **Speaking:** Verbally Inviting Sexual Intimacy **Touching:** Caressing, Cuddling, Hugging, Kissing, Sexual / Sensual Touch
Positive	**Being:** Holding Space for Others **Speaking:** Words of Appreciation **Thinking:** Gratitude, Showing Faith & Belief in Me
Powerful	**Being:** Elevating Your Feeling State

Desired Feelings	Ways of Loving
Present	**Acting:** Cherishing Through Eye Gazing **Being:** Attentiveness, I am Love, Being Present, Listening from the Heart, Self-Awareness
Protected	**Acting:** Physical Care **Being:** Cultivating Trust **Touching:** Holding Hands, Holding Me When I'm Hurting, Hugging
Proud	**Speaking:** Words of Encouragement, Words of Praise **Touching:** Public Expressions of Affection
Receptive	**Being:** Accepting All of Me, Acknowledging / Allowing Feelings **Thinking:** Curiosity **Touching:** Holding Me When I'm Hurting, Hugging
Reflective	**Being:** Acknowledging / Allowing Feelings, Self-Awareness **Speaking:** Sharing Feelings **Thinking:** Remembrance
Relaxed	**Acting:** Activating Joy & Fun **Being:** Being Present, Cultivating Trust **Touching:** Caressing, Cuddling, Hugging, Massage, Non-sexual Touch, Sexual / Sensual Touch
Release	**Speaking:** Sharing Laughter **Thinking:** Forgiveness **Touching:** Caressing, Cuddling, Kissing, Sexual / Sensual Touch
Relief	**Being:** Surrender **Speaking:** Sharing Laughter **Thinking:** Working with Fear
Resourceful	**Acting:** Accountability/Self Responsibility, Financial Support **Being:** Elevating Your Feeling State
Restored	**Being:** Cultivating Trust, Wholeness **Speaking:** Apologizing, Sharing Laughter **Touching:** Holding Me When I'm Hurting, Massage, Non-sexual Touch, Sexual / Sensual Touch
Respected	**Acting:** Boundaries **Being:** Apologizing, Cultivating Trust **Speaking:** Apologizing. Authentic / Honest Communication, Sharing Feedback with Love **Thinking:** Embracing Differences, Respect for Who I am, Respecting Choices & Desires **Touching:** Public Expressions of Affection

Desired Feelings	Ways of Loving
Responsible	**Acting:** Accountability / Self Responsibility **Being:** Cultivating Trust, Self-Awareness **Speaking:** Apologizing, Authentic / Honest Communication, Sharing Feedback with Love **Thinking:** Caring for Our Anger
Safe	**Acting:** Physical Care **Being:** Boundaries, Cultivating Trust **Thinking:** Caring for Our Anger, Working with Fear **Touching:** Holding Me When I'm Hurting, Hugging
Satisfied	**Being:** Acknowledging / Allowing Feelings, Wholeness **Touching:** Caressing, Cuddling, Holding Me When I'm Hurting, Hugging, Massage, Non-sexual Touch, Sexual / Sensual Touch, Reconnecting with Touch
Seen	**Being:** Allowing Space or Time Alone, Listening From the Heart, Self-Awareness **Speaking:** Asking for What You Want, Sharing Feelings, Words of Appreciation, Words of Praise **Thinking:** Caring for Our Anger, Embracing Differences, Remembrance
Sensual	**Being:** Being Present **Speaking:** Verbally Inviting Sexual Intimacy **Touching:** Caressing, Cuddling, Hugging, Kissing, Massage, Non-sexual Touch, Sexual / Sensual Touch
Sexy	**Speaking:** Verbally Inviting Sexual Intimacy **Touching:** Kissing, Sexual / Sensual Touch
Soft	**Acting:** Kindness **Being:** I am Love, Gentleness, Listening From the Heart, Patience, Vulnerability **Thinking:** Forgiveness **Touching:** Caressing, Cuddling, Hugging, Non-Sexual Touch, Sexual / Sensual Touch
Solace	**Being:** Holding My Center In Love, Holding Space for Others, Listening From the Heart, Vulnerability **Thinking:** Caring for Our Anger, Working with Fear
Stimulated	**Acting:** Supporting Learning & Growth **Speaking:** Verbally Inviting Sexual Intimacy **Thinking:** Curiosity **Touching:** Caressing, Cuddling, Hugging, Kissing Non-sexual Touch, Sexual / Sensual Touch

Desired Feelings   Ways of Loving

Strong   **Acting:** Accountability / Self Responsibility **Being:** Holding Space for Others

Supported   **Acting:** Acts of Service, Physical Care **Being:** Allowing Space or Time Alone, Patience **Speaking:** Words of Encouragement **Thinking:** Caring for Our Anger, Freedom / Room to Explore, Respect For Who I Am, Respecting Choices & Desires, Showing Faith & Belief in Me **Touching:** Caressing, Cuddling, Holding Hands, Holding Me When I'm Hurting, Hugging

Surprised   **Acting:** Activating Joy & Fun, Surprises / Unexpected Gift

Surrender   **Being:** Surrender **Thinking:** Freedom / Room to Explore, Forgiveness

Sweet   **Acting:** Kindness **Being:** Gentleness, Listening From the Heart **Speaking:** Words of Appreciation, Written Words of Love **Thinking:** Gratitude

Tender   **Acting:** Kindness **Being:** Gentleness, Listening From the Heart **Speaking:** Written Words of Love **Thinking:** Gratitude **Touching:** Holding Hands, Holding Me When I'm Hurting, Hugging, Kissing, Public Expression of Affection

Transparent   **Being:** Boundaries **Speaking:** Asking For What you Want, Authentic Honest Communication, Communicating During Conflict, Sharing Feedback with Love, Sharing Feelings, Verbally Inviting Sexual Intimacy

Solace   **Acting:** Supporting Learning & Growth **Speaking:** Verbally Inviting Sexual Intimacy **Thinking:** Curiosity **Touching:** Caressing, Cuddling, Hugging, Kissing Non-sexual Touch, Sexual / Sensual Touch

Treasured   **Acting:** Cherishing Through Eye Gazing **Being:** Recognizing My Inherent Worth, Gentleness, Listening From the Heart **Speaking:** Words of Appreciation, Written Words of Love **Thinking:** Remembrance **Touching:** Caressing, Cuddling, Holding Hands, Hugging, Kissing, Public Expressions of Affection, Reconnecting with Touch

Desired Feelings   Ways of Loving

Trust

Being: Allowing Space or Time Alone, Cultivating Trust **Speaking:** Communicating During Conflict **Thinking:** Freedom / Room to Explore, Working with Fear, Respecting Choices & Desires, Showing Faith & Belief in Me, Working with Fear

Understanding

Being: Accepting All of me, Acknowledging / Allowing Feelings, Holding My Center In Love, Listening from the Heart, Patience, Showing Compassion, Self-Awareness **Speaking:** Asking for What You Want, Authentic / Honest Communication, Reflective Listening, Sharing Feelings, Sharing Stories **Thinking:** Caring for Our Anger, Curiosity, Embracing Differences, Forgiveness

Unity

Being: Accepting All of Me, Wholeness **Speaking:** Apologizing, Authentic / Honest Communication **Thinking:** Non-Judgment, Respecting Choices & Desires

Unquestioned

Being: Allowing Space or Time Alone, Patience, Recognizing My Inherent Worth **Speaking:** Reflective Listening, Sharing Feelings Thinking: Respect For Who I Am

Valued

Acting: Cherishing Through Eye Gazing **Being:** Recognizing My Inherent Worth, Boundaries **Speaking:** Reflective Listening, Words of Appreciation, Written Words of Love, Words of Praise **Thinking:** Embracing Differences, Gratitude. Remembrance, Respect For Who I Am, Respecting Choices & Desires **Touching:** Caressing, Cuddling, Holding Hands, Holding Me When I'm Hurting, Hugging, Kissing, Public Expressions of Affection, Reconnecting with Touch

Warmth

Acting: Kindness **Being:** Acknowledging / Allowing Feelings, Gentleness, Listening From the Heart **Speaking:** Sharing Laughter, Sharing Stories, Words of Appreciation, Written Words of Love **Touching:** Caressing, Cuddling, Holding Hands, Holding Me When I'm Hurting, Hugging, Kissing, Massage, Reconnecting with Touch

Desired Feelings Ways of Loving

Whole	**Being:** Acknowledging / Allowing Feelings, Accepting All of Me, Boundaries, Cultivating Trust, Wholeness, Recognizing My Inherent Worth **Thinking:** Caring for Our Anger, Embracing Differences, Respect For Who I Am, Respecting Choices & Desires
Witnessed	**Acting:** Cherishing Through Eye Gazing **Being:** Acknowledging / Allowing Feelings, Listening From the Heart, Self-Awareness **Speaking:** Reflective Listening, Sharing Feelings, Sharing Ideas & Dreams, Words of Appreciation, Words of Encouragement, Words of Praise **Thinking:** Gratitude, Remembrance
Worthy	**Being:** Accepting All of Me, Cultivating Trust, Patience, Recognizing My Inherent Worth, Wholeness **Thinking:** Forgiveness, Respect For Who I Am, Respecting Choices & Desires

Step 5: List your most meaningful *Ways of Loving.*

My *Ways of Loving* - final selections:

How can you love yourself more knowing these *Ways?*

List the *Ways of Loving* for those close to you.

Relationship to you   Their *Ways of Loving*

A mandala (pronounced\'mən-də-lə\) is a visual representation of the universe. The center of the mandala is a place of serenity, in our case the heart. The heart is accessed by gates at the four ordinal points, North, South, East and West. The center is surrounded by concentric circles which move from the most intimate to the most distant. Learn more about mandalas and see more images of a traditional mandalas here. You can imagine your heart at the center of your life, then those closest to you, then moving outwards towards neighbors, co-workers, acquaintances, and finally strangers. This is your personal love mandala. This is perfect metaphor for the way we experience love. At The Love Mandala we use this symbol both as a way to teach and a structure to help you identify and remember various aspects of expressing love. A mandala is also a complex, symmetrical, geometric shape which is great for coloring, and we're all for that!

About The Author

Laura Smith Biswas is an author, teacher and entrepreneur committed to furthering the revolution of love on the planet in any way she can joyfully participate. She possesses a passion for exploring how to cultivate intimacy and connection in sacred partnership. She is the co-founder of The Love Mandala along with her business partner Stephanie Miller and lives in the Los Angeles area with her daughters. She holds a M.S. in Spiritual Psychology from the University of Santa Monica and a MBA from Yale University.

About The Illustrator

An artist from an early age, Tamara Brown discovered the medium of henna while attending Ohio University for Photography. Henna's symbolism and connection to a millennia-old, chiefly female tradition led Brown to develop her self-taught hobby into a flourishing business. Brown has evolved a new practice called Reiki Infused Intuitive Henna by enfolding her experience as a Reiki Master with powerful henna designs and symbolism for clients while drawing upon intuitive energy healing techniques. Find out more at www.opalmoonhenna.com.